MW00792002

R.J. STEWART
BIOGRAPHY

R.J. Stewart is a Scottish author, composer and musician living in the USA, wherein he was admitted in 1997 as a "Resident Alien of Extraordinary Ability," a category awarded to those with the highest achievements in the arts or sciences.

He has 41 books in publication worldwide, translated into many languages, and has recorded a wide range of music and meditational CDs, plus music for film, television, and theater productions in Britain, Canada, and the USA.

He teaches workshops and classes worldwide, has appeared in numerous films and documentaries, and gives concerts of his original music and songs, featuring the unique 80-stringed concert Psaltery and other instruments.

In 1988 R.J. Stewart founded the *Inner Temple Traditions InnerConvocation*™® program, which consists of a series of ongoing classes, publications, groups, and trained teachers working with spiritual and imaginative themes.

For further information, please visit the Stewart websites:

www.dreampower.com
www.rjstewart.org
www.rjstewart.net
www.innerconvocation.com

COPYRIGHT
R.J. Stewart © 1988 & 2007

First published in the UK in 1988 by Element Books.

This edition published in the USA and UK in 2007
by R.J. Stewart Books.

All rights reserved worldwide.
All rights reserved, no part of this book may be
reproduced or utilized in any form or by any means electronic
or mechanical without permission in writing from the Publisher.
Contact: www.rjstewart.net.

A catalog record for this book is available
from the Library of Congress.

ISBN: 978-0-9791402-3-5

An Inner Temple Traditions InnerConvocation™® publication.

R.J. Stewart Books
P.O. Box 7803
Roanoke, VA 24019
www.rjstewart.net

ADVANCED
MAGICAL ARTS

Visualization, Meditation and Ritual
in the Western Magical Tradition

BY

R.J. STEWART

R.J. Stewart
Books

ADVANCED MAGICAL ARTS
PREFACE TO THE 2007 EDITION

Many people think that *Advanced* means complex and obscure, especially in the field of magical arts. In truth, the advances are always within the individual, rather than limited solely to techniques or hidden knowledge. There are indeed advances in technique in magical arts: there must be such advances, otherwise human consciousness will stagnate and then decline. We live in a time of advance. Just as materialism and modernism advance at a shocking and destructive rate, so do magical and spiritual arts and awareness advance as never before. Only two comparable advances come to mind, that of the Renaissance when magicians (who sometimes laid their lives on the line) sought to restore the wisdom of the ancient world against suppressive religious dogma, and that of the late 19th and early 20th centuries, when the foundations of our current revival were laid by men and women of genius and spiritual vision.

Such advances are with us now, in a new spiral, a higher octave, and will occur in groups that work together, as a result solely of individual independent growth of the members (not through group dependence), and of course, in a wider manner in the collective consciousness. By collective we should understand the consciousness of humanity, but utterly in context. The collective context is that of the place, the land, the planetary zone, and ultimately the living planet and its entirety of living beings. We are a part of that entirety, and cannot work magic without participation within its vast and powerful field of consciousness, energy, and myriad living beings. To suggest otherwise is either ignorance or ego-maniacal folly on the part of the aspiring magician, be he or she a beginner or experienced, novice or advanced adept.

In this second volume of Magical Arts, I sought to build upon the foundation of volume one, *Living Magical Arts*. The primary aim of this second book may appear to be regarding technique when you first read it ... and indeed, there are many methods, skills and forms of magical training described and proposed throughout the book. The inner aim of the book, however, is about something else altogether, something which is greatly assisted by good disciplines and techniques in magical arts, but is quite independent of them. I am referring to guaranteed attuned and specific inner contact. Magic cannot be worked without inner spiritual contact. Advanced magic involves ongoing work with powerful inner contacts and specific orders, temples and inner-world assemblies. Magic, like music or sport, is team work, and advanced magic involves joining one of the major ensembles or teams as a skilled player. Of course, you have to train to build your skills, but in advanced magic (as in music or sport) you arrive with such skills already sharpened, ready to contribute and eager to learn more.

Throughout this book, the practical work is designed to bring you into contact with the Inner Temples, embodied through the Five Mysteries described in the various chapters. When you work with this material, your spiritual awareness will gradually enter into the Mysteries, which are vitally important for all true magical growth. We, as humans and like all other life forms, grow through interaction. In the consensual and often delusional world of human society, we grow through outer interaction. In the spiritual worlds, we grow through participation in realms of attuned and vibrant awareness. In old-fashioned terms, these are the Mysteries and this is discussed in more detail in the main text. Beyond the Mysteries, and inherent within them, are the Inner Temples into which all advanced spiritual work will lead us. The practical forms in this book, such as the visions and ceremonies, have been used extensively in my Inner Temple Traditions groups for the last 20 years and more.

So contact and participation are everything, while will-power and secret methods are nothing. Understand this and you are already on the path to advanced magic. The material in this book was tried and tested for years, both by myself and by groups working in Britain and USA before it was committed to publication. We have done it and it works, not only for us, but for many. It will work for you too, providing you are willing to spend some time and effort. Most of all, you have to stay with it. Breakthroughs into advanced magical arts and abilities often seem to be sudden, even dramatic; but in truth they build slowly, like seeds under the earth with hidden roots at first, which grow up-reaching stems, and then the miraculous appears into the light. Do we dare presume that we are any different?

Both of the Magical Arts volumes were intended for the new magicians of the 21st century, so I am pleased that they are appearing in new editions in this crucial century of potent planetary transformation. Of course, such new magicians are ourselves, and those that come after us, ever renewed and open to spiritual change through the venerable arts of magic. True magic is always undertaken, not only for the present, but for the future. Magic can change the future: skilled and ethical magicians, regardless of culture or tradition, are needed now for the seeding of the future. In the advanced work of this nature we never seek to impose our wishes, idealism or will upon the future. Instead, we work with unconditional compassion and readiness, sensing the planetary changes which flow as vast tides from the stellar world to the lunar world; tides that affect the collective on Earth and which generate deep responses from the planet itself. We work with this tide of Call and Response and with the spiritually advanced inner contacts of the Mysteries and the Inner Temples to allow the forces to flow in harmony, in peace and in beauty. Always participate, never interfere. The rest is magic.

R.J. Stewart
Arcata, California, 2007

CONTENTS

ILLUSTRATIONS

ACKNOWLEDGEMENTS

I would like to acknowledge in alphabetical order the influence and inspiration of the following people, who may never have associated with one another: Frederick Bligh Bond, Dr John Dee, Dion Fortune, W. G. Gray, Dr Deirdre Green, Ronald Heaver, The Reverend Robert Kirk, Professor Anders Nygren, Kathleen Raine, A. E. Waite, W. B. Yeats.

Specific acknowledgements are due to: Dr Gareth Knight, who has discussed with me many aspects of the work found in these pages over the years, and who read and commented upon parts of the manuscript; to Francis Israel Regardie, who suggested some of the developments of new material during 1978, and demonstrated the extraordinary perception of a true adept during what was, on the surface, a casual Californian lunch; to Miranda Gray for her artwork on so many projects.

I must also thank those contemporary workers of magic who willingly and often strenuously undertook, with me, some of the visualisations and ceremonies which led, in part, to the examples published here for the first time.

Finally I should acknowledge the anonymous teacher who first instructed me in meditation almost thirty years ago, and bore my juvenile questions with such patience during our chance meetings in a cathedral.

R. J. Stewart, 1988

PREFACE

There is no claim whatsoever that the material in this book is superior or unique. Indeed, as it is drawn from continuing traditions of magical arts, it cannot claim to be beyond the traditions themselves, though it is aimed at potential development of such traditions for the future.

This is the companion volume to *Living Magical Arts*[1] and some of the concepts and practical work described in that book are developed in detail in the examples of ritual and visualisation in our later chapters. But *Advanced Magical Arts* is also designed to stand on its own, and is for the reader who is dissatisfied with the plethora of beginners' books on magical or esoteric subjects, and who can already meditate, concentrate and visualise. Thus the contents are advanced in the sense that they are for those who wish to move on from the levels usually found in classes, open groups, or publication, particularly in modern lightweight or popularised books. I would personally hope that it will provide some interest for those who have already left such opening stages, even those well trained in magical work, though I would not presume to be able to 'teach' such people anything, merely to provide some alternative material. Any magician will readily admit that he or she cannot teach; magic is learned through experience once the initial stages have been passed; most self-styled teachers tend to repeat what little they have learned rather than brave any further adventures.

The word 'advanced' is also used in the sense of developments in technique and specific content; many of the items selected for publication here were originally 'secret', confined to small groups or individual experiments. There is no time or space wasted in arguing the validity of certain concepts such as the 'reasons' for working magic, the 'reality' of inner dimensions or transpersonal consciousness; these are treated as facts that may be, and probably have been, experienced by the reader his or herself. There are also a number of explorations of the metaphysics and psychology so typical of magic, particularly where it seems that standard published systems which are blindly accepted may be clarified or even disposed of. Much of this aspect becomes evident as the book develops.

Another major aim is to show that it is possible to advance magical arts without any of the customary paraphernalia of multi-cultural languages, mysticism borrowed at several removes from its true context, and obscure reductions or expansions of texts and sets of correspondences deriving solely from literary sources. In other words, this book asserts that there is a strong Western magical tradition which applies to most of the European, American, Canadian and Australian peoples. So much work has been done to reinstate this tradition to its proper role in the last decade, by numerous writers ranging from historians to practising magicians, that it is now possible to show how certain themes, motifs, visionary and cosmological texts and traditions which were virtually ignored by nineteenth-century occultists (with a few important exceptions), can be made to work at advanced levels.

Such truly magical work can only be undertaken once the basic disciplines and skills have been learnt that enable us to put this root material into operation. Therefore this book is prefaced with a mild warning: if are you a complete beginner you may find some of the concepts, visualisations and ceremonial patterns difficult or even disturbing. This is not unnatural, but to be expected: no one would seek to enter into any special skill without training; anyone who did so might run risks through ignorance or lack of fitness. Magic is, to paraphrase the late Dion Fortune, more like athletics than aesthetics.

R. J. Stewart, 1988

READER'S GUIDE TO USING THIS BOOK

The text is arranged in two main parts. The first is devoted to theory and discussion of practical applications of theory. Much of the subject matter in Part One is essential to understanding, using and developing that of Part Two, which contains examples of visualisations and ritual or ceremonial texts and patterns.

Each of the main chapters has a number of subheadings, which will enable the reader, to a certain extent, to study sections briefly without working through the entire chapter. But it must be emphasised that magical arts do not work in an encyclopaedic or sectional manner; all parts are reflected and attuned to one another. This poses considerable problems when writing or reading a book on magical traditions and practices, and to this day no author has fully resolved the difficulty, due to the linear nature of the written word.

A proven method of use is to read the entire book from cover to cover, as if it were a novel, taking no notes, and attempting no practical examples. As we are dealing with magical matters, motifs and methods which stimulate and transform awareness through a cycle or holism of symbols, an intellectual or rigorous study approach inevitably fails to gain results. Such discipline, however, is essential and invaluable as one stage or controlled aspect of study and experiment, and we abandon it at our peril. Thus the first reading of magical books, be they medieval or modern, is a process of simple absorption.

The Visualisations

In the case of the present book, I would then recommend the reader to begin work immediately with the Visualisations, with reference to the key chapter on the Five Mysteries and their relationship to one another. Each visualisation has relevant introductory material, and the Merlin sequence has a detailed commentary after the text. By the time each visualisation has been experienced, it may be helpful to return to Part One, read it again in detail, and take any notes or make individual written conclusions and comments for future use.

The Rituals

The Rituals should be approached only after experience with the Visualisations; they are all powerful ceremonies requiring a degree of skill, humour and ruthless dedication. No magician can survive or develop without these qualities; our courage may fail temporarily, our faith waver, our trust in others be abused; but without ruthless dedication to developing skills in the art, and without the most important ability to laugh at ourselves occasionally, everything founders.

The Ritual texts are intentionally presented in different ways:

1. The first example, the *Ritual of the Son of Light*, is supported by an introduction, detailed commentary, and has optional expansion sections using Celtic archetypes or god-forms.
2. The second example, the *Incantation*, is a very different type of text, in the tradition of those incantations employed by the magician who works alone. There are a few notes on the practical aspects of this text as a ceremony.
3. The third example is an adaptation of a specific group ritual which has been regularly worked. The text works within the *Mystery of Merlin*. It is a fairly complex ceremony, particularly in the use of personae from legend, but apart from a short introduction no notes are given. One of the hallowed instructional methods in magic is that not all material should be continually supported by exposition; there is always the danger that continual explanation will condition responses, and will weaken the originality of root material such as visualisations or ritual pattern-making.
4. The last example is a ritual based upon the *Mystery of the Weaver*.

INTRODUCTION

Background and Concepts

This book contains practical material for advanced work within the Western esoteric or magical tradition: it also discusses theoretical aspects of such work, and makes definitions concerning the mainstream tradition within Western consciousness, and its various branches or sub-traditions. But it is not intended as an exhaustive or academic survey of the field, for the emphasis is always upon practical work. Practical magic is undertaken through ritual pattern-making, visualisation and long-established arts in which controlled use of the imagination and personal or group energies are employed for the purpose of transformation.

The nature and value of such transformation are discussed and defined throughout the remainder of this book; it forms one of the major aspects of magical arts, mystical insight, and, in the materialist sense, psychology. Magical psychology, however, is different in many ways from modern restatements, definitions and methods of rebalancing the psyche. Perhaps the most significant difference is that, despite many regional or historical differences, magical and mystical psychology has a foundation and educational experience which has endured for thousands of years, using a symbolic language which on its highest levels transcends creed or culture. Materialist psychology, by comparison, is a derivative and limited side-study, still in its merest infancy.

We should add here that the inner and outer transformations so essential to magical arts may not be subject to rigid definition: on the simplest level this is demonstrated by the obvious though misleading concept of 'subjective' experience, in which the same apparent event may have very different inner values for separate individuals. The definitions offered in this book, therefore, are not regarded as rigid or immutable but as general guides and guardian concepts.

As with all genuine inner or spiritual traditions, magical arts have been developed through vast cycles of experience and experiment ranging over many cultures and practical schools, religions, orders or Mysteries. The initially subjective variations in results (encountered during early training or experimentation) are due to the different horizons, starting-points and psychic patterns of participating individuals. There are, however, coherent results shared by students of all levels who persist within their chosen tradition or magical school of training; such shared and attested experiences eventually merge with archetypical modes of consciousness.

These archetypical modes or levels are modified and mediated by any school or tradition, but are ultimately universal. Thus we have a situation in magical work whereby the earliest stages seem to be highly 'subjective' and to vary enormously from person to person; the middle stages frequently show a surprising and sometimes dramatic coherence of experience and imagery shared by groups and by physically separate individuals; the higher stages transcend individuality and also move beyond controlled or symbolic structures that may be shared, so entering into areas of consciousness that seem paradoxical to our habitual conditioned outer awareness.

Once a group or an individual is attuned to the mainstream of a tradition in magical arts, the random aspect of inner reactions rapidly changes, and with discipline certain defined stages of consciousness may be attained. But this too is an experience that passes, for there is no guaranteed blueprint or directory of esoteric transformations, despite the desperate obsessions with such devices that are found in so many books on magic. Beyond the broad patterns defined by tradition, there are realms of consciousness, states of energy, in which metaphysical laws may operate in paradoxical ways: advanced magical arts work directly with traditional material to reach into these realms of consciousness and energy.

The word 'advanced' has been chosen to describe many aspects of magical arts found in this book, but advanced does not imply superior or élitist or self-inflated claims for either the author or the material. *Advanced Magical Arts* sets out to offer to the reader, and most of all to the practising student, potential and actual material that is not generally available.

There are a vast number of books on meditation, concentration and the basics of magical arts; many are mere journalism, copying from copies in an ever increasing set of repetitious basic manuals for assumed novices, aimed at the non-existent stereotype of the man and woman in the street (beloved of publishers and television programmers), or the generally indiscriminating beginner, the type of person so familiar to unscrupulous 'teachers' who charge money for their blandishments.

Even more disturbing than this rash of relatively trivial literature is the undertone found in many books, by which we may detect subtle hints that the authors have not actually worked to any real extent with magical arts. Some writers merely condense or copy from other larger works; some dash off the most frivolous nonsense in which the lack of actual magical experience and skill is only matched by the absence of essential (even if minimal) historical and cultural research. It should be stated that there are social groups, societies, magazines, and individual persons who have associations (sometimes long-standing) with magical arts, yet never contact any genuine transformative or effective tradition. This superficial level may have a certain value in its own right, for it acts as a net for students who prefer lighter social activities to the demanding disciplines of enduring esoteric training; more subtly, such organisations and self-acclaiming teachers help to show us exactly what magical arts are not.

There is also a deeper spiralling level of this type of experience, for there are a number of what might be loosely termed 'negative teachers', individuals who set themselves up to teach and lead students, yet actually have a limiting, repressive, and unhealthy influence. Many students have to undergo such a negative contact before moving on to levels of work that are their true occupation and endeavour: so in a curious sense warped or corrupted teachers still serve the higher aims and intentions of spiritual development.

By contrast to the ever increasing range of popular and journalistic commercial books, we have the vast systems and productions of the nineteenth century, which still form the unquestioned basis for many modern publications. Much of this material derives from Masonic symbolism, fused with the indiscriminate enthusiasm for the novel and the exotic that ran through late Victorian and early Edwardian society.

Since the development, flourishing and virtual decay of Victorian theosophy and intentionally magical orders such as the Golden Dawn or various derivatives, a steady development in Western magical arts has been taking place. A small number of influential writers represent this development, though there are undoubtedly other practitioners of the art who never venture into publication or public tuition, who are equally or perhaps more influential. This development has been particularly powerful and rapid during the period between the 1960s and the 1980s, and is not necessarily related to the highly intellectual and essentially literary work that is often stated (without any real research or evidence) to be the authoritative Western tradition. We may see the period from the middle of the century to its end (1960–2000) as a time of gradual catalysis and definition of magical art; much of the frivolous nonsense from the post-War era of false liberation, which at first acted as a corrective to the dull, egocentric, male-dominated magical orders of the preceding generations, is being disposed of. The more profound levels of metaphysics and magical training inherited from the nineteenth century present a more complex problem.

The arguments both for and against the validity of systems such as the vast Golden Dawn Anglo/Hebraic/Oriental corpus of rituals and symbols are long and often tedious, but it is sufficient to state here that there are powerful and enduring Western traditions that make no use of Hebrew attributes or Eastern terminology such as are found extensively in nineteenth- and early twentieth-century texts stemming from the Victorian revival of occultism. These sources, frequently ignored by, or even unknown to, nineteenth-century European revival occultists have been particularly valuable and effective in development of magical work and training.

It is important to note that the Western magical or esoteric systems of lore referred to often relate closely to early sources containing Celtic traditions, to classical sources from both Rome and Greece, and to a number of medieval texts and traditions. The medieval sources are not necessarily those much-publicised and little-understood *grimoires* that delighted literary researchers into the obscure and romantically dangerous, but quite a different and much greater body of work. This was assembled by various writers, bards, poets, and chroniclers or historians from what might be termed organic or collective traditional material. This body of work contains, despite its anonymous collective foundation in oral tradition, surprisingly individual and significant elements of alternative symbolism, particularly in its fusion of pagan and primal Christian belief and practice. To put it into simpler terms, we may find potent magical material in those texts which act as thresholds between the old oral tuition of early societies, and the later written and rigidified systems which led to the growth of materialist science and the exteriorisation and ultimate devaluation of the imagination as a moving force in human life. The power of these threshold texts survives translation and cultural change – though caution is always essential.

These diffuse but curiously coherent sources contain no vast edifices of 'authority or 'complete systems' as they derive from collective traditions rather than individual intellectual effort or any formalised hierarchical body. Although a relatively small number of inter-cultural elements are naturally or innocently present, the texts to which we refer contain no vague or confusing rationalisations of Eastern or Hebrew terminology and mystical systems. Such oriental systems, potent in themselves but so frequently parroted and misrepresented by European writers suffering from the grand delusion of rational analysis and European superiority, really should play no part in a genuine Western magical tradition or system of training. There are, however, many potential sources for symbolism, lore and tuition that are close to the centre or foundation of Western consciousness. If we are able to restate such material for modern use, we side-step many of the unnecessary convolutions of Victorian occultism on one hand, and the vast inheritance of religious psychological propaganda and suppressive dogma on the other.

Between these two guardian monsters, there is a path of magical inner development which is well represented both by systems and certain enduring images or legendary magical persons. Perhaps the most obvious and best-known example is that of Merlin,[2] who far from being an ancient magician (as he is popularly described) began his career as a prophetic youth, became a wild man of the woods living close to nature, and finally retired to contemplate divinity as a wise elder. Such lore, hardly touched upon in general occultism, is found in detail in the works of Geoffrey of Monmouth (twelfth century), who drew in turn from bardic and classical traditions preserved and disseminated actively by story-tellers during his own lifetime.

It is from sources of this kind – and the Merlin texts are only a fraction of the lore available – that we may derive truly original or potential material for advanced magical arts rather than from experimental and often misleading literature of the last century, in which great intellects and romantic characters were groping their way, justifiably and often effectively, out of sterile materialism and dogmatic religion. Yet such pioneers could never be free of the yoke of state religion: they could hardly imagine magical arts without an *authoritative* Hebrew/Christian background or alphabet. Like the Philosophers' Stone, there is a wealth of native material lying freely available to us all, yet like the deluded alchemists or puffers we seek in every exotic and complex manner and place for what which is right in front of our noses. There is no suggestion, however, that we delve into increasingly rare manuscripts as a sole source of Western magical arts; the famous legend collections and the rare sources alike have to be enlivened by practical work, otherwise they are mere curiosities, no matter how much valuable lore and symbolism they contain and preserve. Tuition within the Western magical tradition comes from inner sources, not manuscripts or books or even human teachers; sources of tuition are only found through meditation, visualisation and ritual pattern-making. We have to work with our material, rather than merely select, read and comment upon it.

The social and political transformations in Europe and America during this century, resulting from two massive wars and an astonishing acceleration of technology, indicate very deep changes of collective consciousness. Many of the older-style methods and rituals of occult orders now seem dull, highly egocentric and melodramatic, and occasionally fraught with terrible ignorance. No doubt much material of the occult revival from the 1950s to the year 2000 will seem similarly poor to the magicians of the next century, but each period of change in our culture brings forth its own revival of esoteric arts and disciplines according to its own needs.

While overall transformations within any esoteric tradition are collective and organic, there are always individual researchers (who may not be authors or teachers) who leap far ahead of our general understanding of those higher modes of consciousness and vital energies which form the central themes of all magical arts. Such far-reaching magicians are not necessarily known by name, but are certainly represented in legend and tradition by specific personae, just as the world religions have specific saints or holy men and women who may or may not have existed physically, but ultimately develop mythical or allegorical attributes through long association and actual visualisation or inner contact.

Historical biography of such people is ultimately valueless; they have left the trivia of one individual lifetime behind and become something more than human as an inspiration, or even as a warning, to those who seek to follow them upon the path of irrevocable transformation. There is a growing trend in present-day publication towards endless, often superficial, biographies of famous or infamous magicians and teachers, in which the reader's attention is focused upon a type of vicarious thrill at details of the outer life, rather than upon the depth of inner work undertaken by the magicians themselves.

The classic subject of this type of journalism is of course Aleister Crowley; writers revel in his eccentricity, egomania and drug addiction, and in his dissolute and apparently failed life. Yet no modern reassessment of his work has been seriously attempted, despite the fact that many of his books and his remarkable tarot deck are projects of major significance, even with all their flaws and the deliberate posturing and offensiveness of the author. It has frequently been observed that if Crowley had been active in the liberation drug culture of the 1960s (where he seems really to have belonged) he would have commanded far less attention for his weaknesses and perhaps more for his undeniable strengths.

Even Dion Fortune, the most profoundly influential female occultist since the charismatic and enigmatic Madame Blavatsky, has been subjected to the pale, sickly light of superficial biography by various writers. Yet she repeatedly asserted in her novels (which contain her most advanced teaching) how ephemeral the personality and details of one lifetime are in contrast to the overview and timeless consciousness developed through magical arts.

Some Preliminary Definitions

Advanced magical arts are not necessarily the strenuous, obscure undertakings that we might think; in many cases advanced work with transformative inner disciplines is remarkably simple. But the magician has undergone a firm training before such simplicity may be achieved, so we may make some preliminary definitions before proceeding to theory and practice in the form of specific visualisations and rituals.

The developing practitioner of advanced magical arts must have grounding and experience in the following disciplines: meditation, concentration, visualisation and ritual pattern-making. No advanced work may be undertaken without training and experience in these four skills. There are five fundamental arts or disciplines in magical work, and the first four tend to lead towards the fifth, which is *mediation*.[1]

Mediation is the only fundamental of the five essential disciplines or arts that is not a firm prerequisite for advanced work. In many cases the developing magician will have experience of mediation, but it is possible (and in some ways advisable) to assemble a magical group in which well-trained officers or operatives use their skills in the first four arts to build energy and supporting symbolic patterns for those skilled or talented in mediation. The combined result is ritual and mediation of a very high level of power, resulting from the balanced co-operation of skills and forces; yet this traditional system is becoming increasingly unsuitable to modern requirements in magic.

In the case of the individual magician, mediation is often undertaken as part of higher visualisation and meditation, in which the transformed consciousness, guided by imagery, assumes (takes upon itself) the energies and qualities of a chosen god- or goddess-form. This is one of the most ancient and enduring inner disciplines, and should not be confused with any trivial notions of self-inflation and aggrandisement such as occur in mental or emotional imbalance.

In early magical training there is a vast blurred area in which personal weaknesses and problems become highly amplified before they are destroyed and their energies absorbed into a balanced inner pattern. Large orders or organisations in the cultures of the past were often able to utilise this phase, in group rituals, to enable powerful mediation through novices, using the weaknesses as lines of least resistance for higher energies or entities. This type of operation is most inadvisable and potentially dangerous today, as there are no supportive cultural, religious or magical structures able to handle such methods. To balance this, we must always remember that the merest beginner in magical arts, or in any school of spiritual development, may experience powerful changes of consciousness. At its deepest level this occurs within innocent individuals who have no accumulated rigid psychic patterns to obstruct or warp the deeper levels of power. The popular nonsense about the value of virgins in magical ritual is based upon a gross misunderstanding or wilful perversion of this spiritual and magical law.

We need to be cleared of our imbalances before undertaking advanced magical work, at least to a level where we do not delude ourselves concerning the forces that we seek to mediate. In early work individuals often become romantically or even dangerously confused by the mediation or influence of powerful images and entities (god- and goddess-forms, innerworld masters and other independently conscious forms that exist upon imaginal dimensions). In advanced work we understand that while mediation is sometimes a total experience, it is always temporary, and never a matter of personal inflation or superiority. Indeed, true mediation is always accompanied by a disturbing echo of undeniable deep personal insight; it often indicates areas of weakness that require inner attention and development or rebalance. In this role alone, work such as mediation of advanced forms of consciousness or god- and goddess-forms is of immense value to us, though its resulting personal insight is only one of many side-effects and not a major aim.

The major aims of effective mediation are, of course, defined by the pattern of any ritual or visualisation in which assembled energies are given unusual form and direction. *Unusual* does not imply *unnatural*, but magical arts worldwide rest upon the premise that energies may be assembled and directed into patterns which are not customary or random: advanced magical arts reach further and further into patterns that are traditionally taught as being the prime matrices for universal energy and consciousness; thus we might say that such work realigns energies that have become out of phase with higher orders of pattern, or with spiritual consciousness. This is a perennial magical aim.

The higher order patterns, archetypes, or matrices, are traditionally taught as constants, or as undergoing changes of shape over such vast periods of outer time (equivalent to stellar time-scales) as to be imperceptible to individual human consciousness. In the human world, and in the innerworlds which form a major part of all magical experience and practical work, the great matrices or universal archetypes (very different from the 'archetypes' of modern psychology or the anthropomorphic forms found in myth and legend) are used as ritual patterns. They appear as cosmologies, glyphs, maps and simple but potent symbols. Such symbols endure throughout magical training, from the simplest beginners' exercises to the most advanced and specific use of energies for chosen ends. They include the great glyphs such as the Tree of Life, the Fourfold Circle or Wheel of Life, the Hexagram, the Pentagram and other flat representations of the metaphysical or Platonic forms.

The difference between advanced magical arts and early training lies in the way in which the glyphs are employed, particularly in the routing and polarising of energies between human magicians and the innerworld entities or visualised forms employed to focus the force raised by the ritual itself.

Aims of Advanced Magical Arts

In the broadest sense the aims of magical arts persist through all levels from the outset to advanced work. But advanced magical arts often concentrate upon specific subjects, while initial work consists of general training, theory and practice which will in time enable the student to undertake well-defined projects. Before proceeding further, we need to be clear upon apparent differences between the spiritual aims of magical art, and the specific projects or phases which are found within that broad overall aim towards spiritual development.

Firstly we need to remember the basic definition that magic is an artistic science that seeks to transform any given subject or object through the use of controlled energies. The deepest aim of magical arts is to use the fundamental disciplines within one's self to reach towards spiritual maturity and enlightenment;

magic employs powerful, often cathartic changes to this end, unlike the broader, more gentle methods used in religious devotion or the increasingly popular practice of general meditation.

While mass religion relies almost entirely upon faith and grace to gain spiritual insight, enlightenment and potential transformation, the magician undertakes a serious training programme, but does not necessarily lose his or her recognition of faith and grace. Although strong denials are made, there can be no doubt that technically all religious monastic orders and specialised forms of training for priesthood are based upon the fundamental arts and disciplines that underpin magic worldwide. Thus we should remember that advanced magical arts are no different in form or material from basic training in the five fundamental arts or disciplines; it is merely that the energy employed is often of a higher level and more effectively directed. In this sense advanced magical work serves the same primal purpose as any method of inner transformation, to reach towards and realise a higher transcendent or spiritual reality and consciousness.

In each cycle or era, however, advanced magical work tends to concentrate upon specific aims; once individual skills have been developed to a certain level, they are often employed upon clearly defined projects. While specific project-orientated work may assist the spiritual growth of the group or individual, it does not necessarily have this deepest of concepts as its major aim, just as a concert performance does not necessarily improve the technique of a musician, but is aimed at a collective end and attempts the finest utterance of a chosen work of music. In other words, advanced magical work assumes that we work constantly upon our technique and abilities, and puts them to use in collective projects.

It should be emphasised that these are *magical* projects, which do not necessarily emerge as social or political movements, though very often there appear to be certain interplays between outer and inner patterns. This interplay is often confusing or even disturbing to magicians, especially if they avoid their true magical discipline and become embroiled in fruitless politics. If we allow for a lapse of time, which often may not be pre-defined, the general culture often catches up materially or socially with concepts that were once the property and work of magicians.

The greatest example is of course materialist science, which emerged from the experiments of the alchemists and the later magicians of the Renaissance; they were prepared to experiment with new concepts and disciplines in pursuit of knowledge and enlightenment even while such experiments were deeply disapproved of by the religious authorities, by government and by society in general. Psychology, another interesting example, has availed itself of those techniques of ancient magical and religious disciplines that led to inner perception, and transformed them into an acceptable form of therapy for our materialist society. A third example (and many more could be added) is awareness of the environment, which occupied the efforts of a number of magical orders at a time when Western society generally was happy to pollute and destroy in a frenzy of development and greed. Environmental awareness and protection is now a serious political matter, but we should never lose sight of the fact that it is also an ethical and ultimately spiritual matter, which is the position from which magical groups have always worked.

What, therefore, would the aims of advanced magical arts be? If we were to be specific rather than general, what rituals and aspects of mediation (rather than meditation) would a group or individual undertake in the twentieth to twenty-first centuries? Given that initial training and skills in the five fundamental arts have been proven, and that it is not necessary to describe, for example, 'how to meditate' or what a ritual may or may not be, a short list of possible projects might read as follows:

1. Increased consciousness of the land and ultimately of the planet.
2. Conscious regeneration of imaginal forms (also known as telesmatic images) for purposes of individual and collective rebalance.
3. Deeper association with innerworlds in pursuit of knowledge and enlightenment.
4. Regeneration and rebalancing of corrupted or unhealthy magical patterns known to be in existence at present. This is not necessarily a matter of 'fighting evil' or any type of righteousness or crusading obsession: very often it consists of reattuning forces

that have become isolated from their proper life-cycle – a type of repairing or maintenance service.

5. Restatement of certain primal mythic themes as active forces within the imagination.

6. The opening and restoration of natural power sites within the environment: related to (1) above but often very localised and specific.

7. Development of new forms and expressions for the energies of magical instruction and inner development.

8. Invoking images and forces of rebalance and harmony into the outer world; these may help to adjust our unhealthy and potentially self-destructive human culture. This concept is radically different to that of wishing or praying for peace and goodwill: it involves specific operations undertaken in a spirit of service or unselfishness. While the deepest aim is identical to that of religion, or indeed of any thoughtful, ethical individual or movement, magical operations always use well-defined images and methods.

The list suggested above is not in any way definitive, nor does it act as a set of proposals or a work plan. It is merely a typical set of objectives found in advanced magical arts, which result in precise operations such as rituals or visualisations with definite ends to attain.

We could take any one of the categories listed and amplify it considerably, formalising some of the concepts and potential projects that might derive from using it as a starting-point. The rituals and visualisations in our later chapters fit into one or more of the categories listed, for there is no reason why a carefully constructed magical operation should not serve several purposes simultaneously. Indeed, one of the hallmarks of an advanced ritual is that it reveals aims and objectives which were not considered at the outset, but which have strong harmonic connections to the original intention.

The multifold nature of such magical arts is traditionally demonstrated by illustrations such as our Figure 1, the Three Wheels and Three Worlds.[3] One of the basic premises of magic at all stages of development is that if consciousness and energy may be aroused, transformed or exchanged upon one of the higher metaphysical levels or spirals, then the effects upon the lower or outer world are far greater.

ADVANCED MAGICAL ARTS

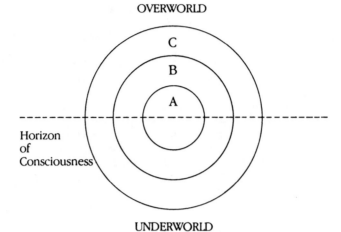

OVERWORLD

Figure 1(a)   The Three Wheels and Three Worlds

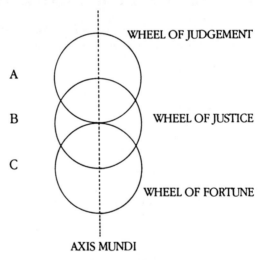

Figure 1(b)   A: Lunar World
B: Solar World
C: Stellar World

If, for example, we are able to build images and concepts in the realm of consciousness known traditionally as the Solar World, and draw these energies through into outer manifestation within the Wheel of Fortune or Lunar and Earth worlds, many of the cycles and rotations of action and reaction (the Wheel of Fortune, the Wheel of Life) are obviated and the energy is not dissipated through customary cycles or accumulations and restrictions which would otherwise limit its effect.

A more subtle practical teaching, not given enough attention in texts on magic, is that the energy or consciousness of higher states or worlds will automatically trigger many potential paths of interaction in our outer world. The force flows through whatever paths are available to it: the forces of the deepest (analogous to highest) worlds, states or dimensions of consciousness/energy will trigger many effects.[4] The effects triggered vary from inner transformations in the magician or group, to collective organic changes in general consciousness. In specific rituals, energy from the higher worlds often activates symbol systems, locations or images that have lain dormant for long periods of time.

One of the typical projects of advanced magical arts is to activate such nexus points or images and establish their nature and purpose, and of course their general state of health. They are then either reinstated to full operation in keeping with the present culture and future aims, or closed down. In rare cases it may be essential to seal or even destroy a power focus (such as the inner aspect of a natural site or a magical image) but such operations are very rare indeed, particularly in the context of natural power sites, which usually work on multifold levels and for varying purposes. Much of the popular nonsense regarding so-called 'exorcisms' and the transforming of 'evil' pagan sites is merely wishful thinking on the part of would-be magicians or evangelists, or at its worst it is pernicious journalism and suppressive propaganda.

The general level of work undertaken by experienced magicians is often high but intentionally limited; romantic notions of world transformation tend to be left behind in advanced magical arts.

PART ONE

1

THE FIVE MYSTERIES

Specific Mysteries in Magical Arts

All examples in this book, ritual texts or visualisations, are
attuned to specific Mysteries. This means that anyone working
with the material seriously will be likely to come into contact
with certain inner realities which lead to transformation. The
term *Mystery* is used to describe a clearly defined and ordered
school of magical and spiritual development that exists upon
inner levels. This is an extension of the historical definition of a
Mystery (such as the classical Eleusinian or Orphic Mysteries or
any of the mystical, magical and spiritual schools of esoteric
tuition known throughout the ancient world).

By this extension of the term, we approach the real heart of
the concept; a Mystery is not merely a historical, cultural
occurrence to be catalogued by academic journalists and
republished in fragmentary form. Just as the classical Mysteries
were advanced or esoteric schools that went beyond formal cults
or religions, so are the inner Mysteries a metaphysical reality
beyond their outer schools. When we admit that the outer
schools are long since demolished and lost, it is only upon an
inner level, through meditation, visualisation, ritual pattern-
making and spiritual intuition, that we may approach the
Mysteries.

When we do so, we find that there are several highly
interactive schools, Mysteries, or innerworld orders and structures. There is no place in a book on advanced magical arts to
waste space arguing the existence or non-existence of such inner
dimensions and orders: the practical magician seeks to establish

their reality or fiction through actual experience rather than through literary or social debate.

In this experiential context, the material of our rituals and visualisations is, without exception, linked to specific Mysteries. Furthermore, they are the primal, highly effective Mysteries of Western magical tradition, which pre-date and in many ways supersede the familiar, mainly literary, concepts found in modern magical texts from the nineteenth century onwards. There are many connections in our examples to standard systems of magical training that are well published, but the Mysteries selected for this book (and there are many that could have been chosen) are fundamental structures found in Western tradition.

It must be stressed that no matter how much modern support (or antipathy) is given to material such as the Golden Dawn system, or the comprehensive works of Aleister Crowley and other modern occultists, these do not comprise a root tradition; very often they are totally out of contact with Western magical tradition, particularly when they employ Eastern lore out of context and without the writers having had genuine experience of Eastern culture, philosophy or religion.

We need only to imagine a situation in which, say, a Chinese magician begins to incorporate Swedish terminology into his texts, with aspects of Scandinavian culture and religion which he has never experienced, even using obscure Swedish traditions and terms, from inaccurate translations and second or third remove texts, which in their original uncorrupted form are only understood by a tiny minority of Swedes. Of course, in our fanciful Chinese context, these Scandinavian mystical items may seem alluring, romantic, mysterious; but they have very little validity for our magician's spiritual development, culture and true oriental spiritual traditions. Does it all seem absurd? Yet this is precisely the situation that most Western magicians are in, for they work with texts assembled in exactly such a manner. The argument developed in the nineteenth century, particularly by the Theosophical Society (which had a profound influence to both good and bad effect upon Western culture), that there was no real Western esoteric tradition and that all wisdom had to come from other sources, is now void and ridiculous.

On a more serious technical note we need only make the obvious comparison (commented upon by a number of writers) between nineteenth-century adaptations of Kabbalah for magical groups, and the true Jewish mystical Kabbalistic tradition.

Enough has been published in both areas for the student to conduct his or her own research: the sad conclusion is that most English-speaking literary occultists with claims to elucidating Kabbalah for non-Jewish students are hopelessly astray. Curiously we occasionally find that early examples of Kabbalah, and early forms of astrology known in the Middle Ages, are far less prone to this problem: in other words there was a fundamental philosophical and metaphysical similarity of language between 'new' structures appearing via Arabic and Jewish contacts in Europe and the 'old' remnants of Greek, Roman, Celtic and other native traditions preserved during the so-called Dark Ages.

But an ever widening gulf opens out between cultures, philosophy and the language of religions, as Christianity becomes increasingly militant and the Western world increasingly expansionist, materialist, and deluded over its appointed role in planetary history. As each century passes, the primal magical world-views are increasingly suppressed, though there are always specific revivals with varying degrees of success and failure. By the nineteenth century an abyss separates the mentality of the learned European from both his medieval forebear and his Eastern contemporaries. Little wonder, in the face of stultifying materialism combined with moribund State religion, that romantic enthusiasm proliferated over Eastern lore, combined with the conditioning that all Christian and Judaic religious or mystical writings must, by dogmatic definition, be of spiritual value to the entire world (when administered by Europeans). All this confusion reigned when the West had, as it always has had, a rich and profound magical, psychological, mystical and spiritual set of traditions entirely its own, and well suited, even in neglect, to immediate use. Indeed, if one fraction of the effort put into matters Vedantic, Kabbalistic, Egyptian or otherwise theosophic had been applied by occultists to the traditions of their own lands, we might have a radically different situation today in esoteric arts and disciplines.

The foregoing does not prevent us, however, from using a primal Tree of Life, for this ubiquitous glyph is found in many forms worldwide, and not restricted to Jewish Kabbalah alone. In Western tradition it has its expression in the cosmology and magical or spiritual psychology of the *Axis Mundi*, the Tree or

Spindle of the Worlds. This gains expression in tarot, though the standard published systems of allocating trumps are needlessly complex or inefficient due to over-rationalisation and pointless attempts at pan-cultural 'completeness' on the part of pioneering authors. We need only to look at the early cosmologies of the classical and post-classical worlds to find considerable evidence for a simple tarot system that relates to the Axis Mundi.[3]

Functions of the Mysteries

It should be clear from the outset that magical and spiritual Mysteries are not a type of glorified adventure or role-playing game; anyone regarding them in this manner is likely to fail in a true contact, or possibly to run the risk of mental or emotional imbalance when the reality of the game becomes apparent. The experiences gained within any Mystery are stark, hard, profound and permanent. In the ancient world initiates were said to be the living dead, who saw the sun at midnight. This is not lurid romance, but a poetic terminology describing deep changes of consciousness. We must also state that the Mysteries contain great beauty and joy, but that ultimately they reach beyond such reactions into a reality that transcends words.

So a Mystery can teach, enliven and transform: but it also reaches beyond its own form and members, into a spiritual reality. A Mystery is finally a way of approaching Truth; all contents are merely signposts.

The Five Mysteries in this book are defined as follows:

1. *The Mystery of the Weaver*
2. *The Mystery of the UnderWorld*
3. *The Mystery of Merlin*
4. *The Mystery of the Vault*
5. *The Mystery of the Son of Light*

Each Mystery is composed of a number of factors:

1. Primal powers.
2. Personae or telesmatic images.
3. Landscape or environment.
4. Individual structures (such as buildings or locations within the landscape).

Further defining factors that contribute to a Mystery are:

> 5. Temporal or transtemporal location (attuned to past cultures, timeless innerworld environments, future potentials, or a harmonic sequence combining any or all of these factors).
> 6. Otherworld or inner dimensional 'location'. Some Mysteries have a strongly environmental quality, while others are found in worlds or dimensions that are rarely experienced by human consciousness. Many Mysteries combine these factors, leading from an environmental scenario into other worlds. This progression is analogous in many ways to movement of awareness from the Lunar through Solar to Stellar World as shown on the Tree of Life, though no firm rule should be expected to apply. Many Mysteries have what might be termed *Side-Gates*, and these can lead to unexpected dimensions.

Relationship between the Five Mysteries

The five Mysteries which generate our examples are linked in various ways: they correspond broadly to a basic pattern found in magical arts, of four worlds, powers, elements, seasons and so forth linked within or generated out of a unifying spiritual Being or Truth. But we should not expect this connective quality to be rigid or unchanging; one of the most exacting and long-standing disciplines in magic consists of visualising topological relationships, first a flat map, then a simple solid from the flat plan, then increasingly complex solids and additional mathematical dimensions. The Platonic solids are, of course, the central example of this essential metaphysical geometry, and some modern exegeses upon the Tree of Life concern metaphysical geometry and topology.

To meditate upon the Five Mysteries, however, we can begin with a very simple diagram (Figure 2) which has proven fruitful. While we begin by assessing the correspondences intellectually, this glyph can be empowered by visualising the forces, forms and personae inherent in each of its components, and attuning to their relationships. Many connectives are discovered when we begin working upon this higher level of comprehension. A summary of the attributes and their relationships might begin as follows:

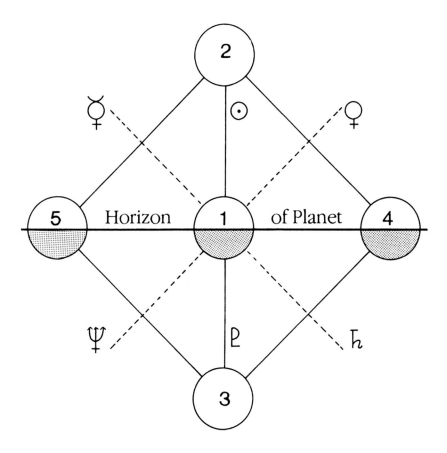

Figure 2   *The Five Mysteries*
    1 *The Weaver*
    2 *The Son of Light*
    3 *The UnderWorld Initiation*
    4 *The Vault*
    5 *Merlin*

The Ground or Horizon line. In the most direct sense this is a line of polar relationship, Above and Below. Thus it corresponds to the mutually reflective concepts of the OverWorld and Under-World, to the obvious analogy of above and below ground which seems simple but was of vital importance to the magic of our ancestors. On a more sophisticated level, still of vital importance to our ancestors who spent thousands of years marking star positions with stones, is the further analogy of the horizon. An alignment of stars to horizon is metaphysically a reflection of powers or events both above and below the earth, or without and within any defined boundary. This concept is extremely important in magic; it is a practical working proposition which is vital to our understanding of the development of astrology, metaphysics, meditation and many other esoteric arts. It also transforms our understanding of the ancient world-views, and if it can be regenerated within our own living awareness, leads to powerful magical abilities.

The vertical line relates Right and Left, or the polar opposites that are, paradoxically, reflections of one another. We shall return to this when we consider each Mystery and its position upon the glyph.

From this very simple basis we could amplify a series of increasingly complex connectives and attributes; this stage, however, is one of refinement upon a personal or specific project level. Thus stellar correlations might be made, or astrological, or psychological, and so forth. The concept works very well indeed in practical magic when it is located upon an environmental power site, and of course it may be applied to the magical room or temple or to the energy field of an individual or group. But such working refinements are based upon five fundamentals, which are outlined below.

1. *The Weaver.* Represents the originative power of Being working through an archetypical matrix (Mother Form). She is both above and below the earth/horizon, for she emits and weaves all forces and forms that comprise all worlds; She is the Goddess Above and Below, of stars and of darkness; as she is both within and upon the earth she is also the Earth Mother of Life, Death and Rebirth. Thus She is both the centre and circumference, inner and outer limit of our glyph. The Weaver is central to a most powerful Mystery upon inner levels, connected to ancient Goddess religions in a historical sense, and to extremely effective transformative energies and entities in terms of ritual, meditation, visualisation and, of course, mediation.

2. *The Son or Daughter of Light.* In our working presentation, the second Mystery is that of the Son of Light. This divine image incorporates and emits all historical religious or mythical examples of Saviours, Redeemers, Enlighteners, Solar Heroes, Sacred Kings. We might equally approach this Being as a feminine archetype, for it is genuinely androgynous, being beyond the polarity of sexual definition as humans understand and experience such matters. The effect of attuning our imagination to masculine or feminine archetypes in this context is a matter that will be highly developed in magical arts of the future, and which has not been given sufficient attention or understanding in the West due to our cultural problems deriving from mono-sexual religious conditioning. Modern goddess-orientated cults and movements are the first signs of a deep ferment of transformation.

In our present context, the Son of Light is defined simply because we have the Mother Weaver as the source and sum of Being. Furthermore inner traditions have employed the male polarity for this spiritual power for millennia; he is the Son of the Mother (not a usurper or jealous god). When we enter into the Mystery, we find that his first appearance is usually male, though this may change several times in the course of a ritual or visionary experience. The outer analogy is to the Sun, which is above the horizon for a proportion of each day, but which moves below in a definable pattern, and is the heart or light-giver of the solar system.

Thus the Son of Light has a zenith position (2) in our glyph or map, but moves around the Four Threshold Mysteries. His nadir position (3) is in the UnderWorld, which is of course a mirror image of his zenith. This concept corresponds to many myths, religious motifs, and to seasonal and solar observations rooted upon ancestral levels of consciousness. Note that we say *ancestral consciousness* and not cultural history; this level of consciousness is still fully present, though buried, in modern humanity, and magical arts break the barriers between this level and outer awareness, in addition to reaching into the transpersonal higher modes or altered states of consciousness.

The Son of Light may be said to move through the Four Thresholds, but these Mysteries also inter-relate as shown upon the glyph. In traditional terminology we would say that each of the Five Mysteries contains an entity, archetype or form for spiritual power. The power is transtemporal, but specific examples (sometimes incarnations) are seeded into the solar cycle and partake of the relative experience of time. Thus we have the myths of solar heroes who descend to the depths in quest of magical benefits, or the universal theme of a Saviour who is made incarnate on Earth, and liberates each of a cycle of other worlds through his or her appearance within them. Magical traditions affirm that considerable attention was given to incarnations of special beings in the ancient Mysteries, and that many of the Goddess cultures of past ages perpetuated cycles of breeding, birth, death and rebirth, over immense periods of time. This is part of the central Mystery of the Weaver, as it manifests in our organic human world.

3. *The UnderWorld*. Below the ground, below the horizon, are the dark potencies and powers. These are not 'evil', but the essential reflections of spirit within matter, or stars within stones. No magical work can be truly developed without experience of the UnderWorld. Furthermore it is the Western *Shortened Way* still preserved in story, song, legend and, most important of all, in practical experience as a rapid method of spiritual enlightenment.

4. *The Vault*. This is a threshold or transitional Mystery, for it rests within the horizon, and partakes of both Above and Below. It represents part of the cycle of the Redeemer or Son of Light, but also acts as a state or place in which humans may gain enlightenment *en route* to or from the UnderWorld or Over-World. It represents, in psychological terms, the transpersonal consciousness or spirit undergoing pupation or practical operations of change prior to emerging in a new condition. The polar partner/opposite to this Mystery is that of Merlin.

5. *The Mystery of Merlin*. This transitional Mystery also rests within the horizon, partaking of both Over and UnderWorlds. But while the Vault defines powers of pupation and rebirth through sacrifice, the *Mystery of Merlin* begins upon an entirely human level. Though we are accustomed to finding Merlin represented as an archetypical (or stereotypical) wise old man, he has three faces: *Bright Youth, Mad Prophet, Wise Elder*. The

Merlin texts define this triplicity in great detail, and it was clearly part of bardic druidic teaching. Merlin is, in fact, the Fool of tarot, who in time becomes the Hermit. *The Mystery of Merlin* is instructional, psychological, cosmological and prophetic. It covers the spiralling transitions from questioning humanity to wisdom and understanding through experience. Thus we may indeed apply to the image of the Aged Merlin in visualisation or ritual, but the Mystery is only truly effective if each of the Three Images are given equal attention.

Study of associated legends will show how the Merlin cycle reflects that of the Son of Light: Merlin is a spiritual child, he goes underground and utters prophecies, he is (in early versions) subject to the Threefold Death of ritual sacrifice and so forth.

Merlin, therefore, is both the prophet and the major teaching master of Western esoteric tradition. If we take an overview, we could suggest that the figure of Merlin stands for many teaching or prophetic sources, and has numerous local, national and international reflections and parallels. Yet Merlin is also a distinct individual master, connected particularly to the land of Britain, and we should not lose sight of this fact in a welter of mock universality.

The Connections

It should be clear from the foregoing summaries that each of the Four Threshold Mysteries is closely connected to the others, with two strongly defined zenith and nadir *worlds* and two polarised horizon *worlds*. We can make a number of further connections as follows:

The Vault corresponds to a certain extent to mystical and primal religious experiences and techniques, fusing the Under-World and OverWorld through the presence of the Son or Daughter of Light in the human world.

The Mystery of Merlin corresponds to a certain extent to the magical and chthonic experiences and techniques (nowadays it is fashionable to call these techniques 'shamanistic' regardless of where they are encountered) fusing the UnderWorld and OverWorld through the mediation of traditional visions, initiations and prophetic experiences. It must be emphasised that these two Mysteries, of Merlin and of the Vault, are not antithetic. They are so mutually intertwined through the presence of the Weaver in the centre of all being that they cannot be falsely separated. Illusions or delusions of separation are due to human folly, or even to deliberate corruption and long-term mass conditioning. Further connectives may be found by meditating upon Figure 2.

2

VISUALISATION

Guided Visualisation

Guided visualisation forms a major constituent of advanced magical arts, though it should not be used as a substitution for meditation or ritual pattern-making, for each of the fundamental disciplines should be equally developed.

Enormous interest in visualisation has arisen in recent years, both within and beyond the fields of magic, occultism and mental therapy. This renewed interest has led to a revival of the art. It must be stressed, however, that the revival may still be in its infancy, for the visualising skills of our forebears were greater than our own, especially in the context of our visual imagination which regular television has caused to atrophy or become conditioned to stereotypical images through long repetition.

The visualisations of early cultures were usually embodied in sagas or mythic cycles, in which poetry, song, music, dance and ritual drama were employed to create visions, shared by performers and audience alike, which attuned to the deepest levels of collective consciousness. These traditions of symbolism and myth were preserved in oral story-telling and in what are often vaguely called 'narrative ballads' for many centuries in the West, while in the East epic traditions based upon myth and religion are still active. It was from similar bardic, poetic and story-telling traditions that early chroniclers, such as Geoffrey of Monmouth (twelfth century), drew the legendary lore for King Arthur, Merlin and the highly developed Grail legends which were soon to follow. These literary reworkings represent the thresholds of oral mythic lore entering earliest literature. We have many other European examples such as Norse or Irish sagas and tales, and of course the classical mythology of Greek and Roman culture remains well represented.

A higher level of such collective symbolism was employed in the specialist training of magical arts or priesthood, and within what are often termed the *Mysteries*. Mysteries were originally organised schools of esoteric development which were not publicly open to all comers, but reserved for those who sought enlightenment beyond collective religion or superstition. The tradition of mystery drama was preserved well into the Middle Ages with religious plays that represented orthodox beliefs and Christian legends in a lively form for the people. These dramas did not, of course, have esoteric formal tuition attached to them, but they sought to replace the folk rituals and dramas of paganism which were still widespread, and which have never wholly been exterminated due to their remarkable vitality and depth of significance. The enduring power of the medieval mystery plays is perhaps due to their close attachment to collective roots, to symbols and motifs within the timeless shared consciousness of the people, rather than to their propaganda or dogma.

In modern visualisation we seek to contact and develop advanced levels of consciousness, traditionally the aim of the ancient Mysteries. In this context it is unfortunate that the art has somehow become attached and often wrongly claimed by various schools of mental therapy. Although visualisation is undoubtedly therapeutic, it need not be limited to such basic levels of employment. Ancient Mysteries, either of the classical sort or their counterparts in other areas of the Western world, were often (but not necessarily) connected to well-established outer religions, acting as an esoteric level of the exoteric worship. In modern terminology, the Mysteries employed in magical arts are established upon inner levels, and are encountered through disciplines such as visualisation, meditation and ritual. They are made active and creative, however, by *mediation*, and though they may be related to aspects of formal religion, are not necessarily orthodox.

A great deal of basic work on visualisation has been published, particularly in general books on meditation, magic and 'occult' practices. It is interesting to find that a high standard of visualisation was demanded in esoteric orders even as late as the nineteenth century. Curiously this standard has lowered as the art has become popularised, and although people are generally more aware of the need and ability to visualise, those who undertake the art are very often denied information on the possibilities available to them. Indeed, many of the vapid fantasies that are employed on tapes, in sessions, or found in books would have been regarded with contempt by the visualisers of earlier generations. On a more serious note, the general trend towards pale, cosy imagery and 'relaxed' sequences may be dangerous. Our imagination is strengthened by complex and demanding work; if it is fed pap and insufficiently exercised it decays.

Pathworkings

A curious development in modern esoteric publication and practice is that visualisations are regularly called 'pathworkings'. This is, regrettably, an inaccurate and misleading description. The term *pathworking* derives from nineteenth- and early twentieth-century adaptations of Hebrew Kabbalah; a *path* is a very specific and clearly defined mode of consciousness or power, the fusion of any two Spheres upon the Tree of Life. Pathworking involves the combination of the symbols, angelic names and divine attributes of two connected Spheres (see Figure 3), and these powers, often in anthropomorphic form, are visualised as uplifting the soul into other worlds, states or dimensions. Once again, these states are well defined in traditional Kabbalah, and form part of a vast and highly sophisticated technology or art of advanced metaphysics. Thus while pathworking involves very demanding visualisations, visualisation is not in itself pathworking.

The type of visualisation used in Western magical arts certainly has a complex alphabet of symbols, and is coherent and capable of very high levels of development. Tarot represents one major development and pattern of such symbolism, originally related to an oral cycle of mythic tales, but there are many other elements to visualisation which are encountered through specific teaching traditions and magical practices. If we assume that a certain level of skill in visualising has been achieved, what elements might be combined to create advanced visualisations within a Western esoteric tradition?

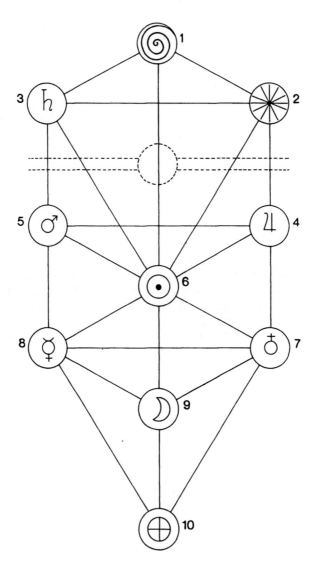

Figure 3   The Tree of Life

Guidelines for Visualisation

Certain general guidelines may be helpful for those who wish to reach beyond the level of pleasant imaginative trips and who are already conversant with the basic symbolic units and images of magical arts. These guides are not rules, but merely directions that are general to the more complex and powerful visualisations used traditionally, and which are encountered and developed during advanced work.

1. The symbolism must be coherent and relate to a specific tradition. Pan-cultural symbols and images are sometimes helpful to broaden the horizons of students, but they do not work on higher or deeper levels of consciousness, due to the collective inherited and environmental laws and images that form the foundation of all magical arts. Significantly, once we have worked fully with a specific tradition and gained skill in its higher or more powerful workings, we can attune to those parallel levels in other traditions, but not until the discipline and painful work of development has been fully undertaken.

2. The visualisation should not be regarded as 'complete' or 'authoritative', nor should the person guiding or writing the sequence attempt to make it all-inclusive. A rigid, highly formalised visualisation is insufficient for the imagination, which always works upon organic and multifold levels of imagery. There should always be paths, routes, images and concepts that are *not* developed, merely stated. These act as potential areas of departure for future work, branches upon the tree of imagery. Such elements often bear a great deal of fruit in meditation, and often act as keys to higher levels of consciousness at a later date. An effective visualisation always steers a careful course, but makes it clear that other courses are indeed possible at any time. The use of subsidiary symbolism (such as doors that are not opened, personae that are glimpsed at a distance, or accesses that are actually denied) may also be employed to point students towards deeper aspects of a tradition or ritual, aspects which may not be stated in words or any obvious symbols, but have to be personally encountered to come alive and act as transformative forces.

3. The sequence and symbols must not be always 'kindly' or 'supportive'. They should be, in part, challenging, demanding and in certain stages daunting or even disturbing. Very little true benefit can be gained from endless jolly, kindly, reassuring dollops of guided imagery (pleasant boat-trips, kindly teachers, wonderful colours, opening flowers, healing rays and the like). These are indeed important units in many types of visualisation, but they are not major ends in themselves. A successful visualisation arouses many aspects of the psyche, and fuses them together in a new energetic pattern. If we do not employ the most potent forces and images, we simply do not reach a higher level of consciousness, but remain upon a pleasant plateau of gentle illusion. This pleasantry may be highly amplified, as in the case of the paradises and heavens of many religions, but it is ultimately a dead end.

4. There should always be opportunities for silent meditation and for people to see inwardly certain visions that should arise if the basic sequence has been properly assembled and conducted. Such visions are usually presaged by innerworld personae or telesmatic images, for these entities act as openers of the inner faculties: the human reader or guide should not presume to open such visionary aspects, as they are the volitional or free properties of individual consciousness, even though they are partly moulded by group imagination within the overall working.

5. Although it is possible to conduct visualisations using personae and situations from popular fiction (regardless of style, quality or reputation) such constructs should be regarded with extreme caution. If we employ traditional imagery, it generates many remarkable sequences and characters for further work: such developments are always grounded within the original tradition, often with surprising results and powerful new forms. Fiction, however, is not necessarily rooted in a magical or spiritual tradition, so in technical terms the images might be called 'impure', particularly where they are laden with supportive sentiment from thousands of enthusiastic readers.

We could cite the important example of the vastly popular works of J. R. Tolkien, which appear to have magical elements, but are actually a massive, complex sequence of reductionism based upon the author's extensive scholarly knowledge of various Western literary texts and sources. The resulting books are pleasant reading, but are horribly imbalanced in terms of sexual polarity and true mystical or magical tradition. In a very strict sense we might even suggest that such works usurp the root traditions of imagery, and move them in an increasingly trivialised direction: other examples of this trivialisation include grotesque popularisations of Arthurian tales, or cartoon parodies of Merlin, and the commercialisation of 'occult' and 'Celtic' themes in popular fiction.

The Fourfold Circle

One aspect of visualisation that has not been given sufficient attention in modern publication and tuition, but was well represented in magical tradition, is that any specific visualisation should bear some structural relationship to magical pattern-making. In other words the movements, directions, location and transformations within the story or imagery of the visualisation should bear some relationship to the precise movements and orientations found in ritual magic. This relationship need not be rigid or overt; stereotypical formality weakens magical art. On a very simple level this general rule may be defined as follows: the progression of a visualisation should be definable upon the Circle (Wheel of Life) or some other important major glyph. (See Figure 4.)

A visualisation should not, therefore, meander through diffuse levels and worlds of imagery and energy. There should be intellectual, psychological, topological and cosmological clarity, through which related realms of consciousness merge, dissolve and re-emerge in a master pattern. This sounds, of course, like a most daunting prospect, and many scholars, adepts and writers have laboured (usually fruitlessly) for years to define an all-inclusive 'complete' master plan for magical arts and symbolism. Like most magical secrets, the answer lies in something learned at the very outset of training; we should be able to place the visualisation, as a pattern or map, upon the Circle, the Three Worlds, or the Tree of Life. This may be undertaken as a secondary or subliminal level while creating the visualisation, or it may be done by drawing up an actual route-map prior to assembling the story of the visualisation

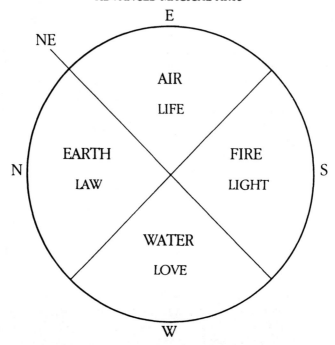

Figure 4   The Wheel of Life and Circle of Magic

itself. Furthermore it should be possible, in most cases, to transpose the visualisation into a ritual pattern upon the basic Fourfold Circle or Circled Cross which is fundamental to practical magic.

We should add that a complex visualisation moves through several levels of consciousness or magical *worlds*. This may be shown upon the Tree of Life, or more subtly through a spherical model which is the proper extension of flat glyphs such as the Circle and Tree. The basis of Western mystical and magical traditions may be shown as three Worlds (Stellar, Solar and Lunar) with the outer or collective world of Earth as the ultimate manifestation of the energies of all three. (See Figure 1.)

Such location and interpretation is an important requirement for advanced magical work; effective magic is capable of multiple forms of expression. In early training the pattern-making (ritual) and imaginal forms (visualisation) need not be deliberately related, though effective tuition should establish this relationship from the outset. Simple visualisations are concerned with restoring the often atrophied visualising ability, then training it to work with specific symbols and images. Only subsequent stages of working need to be related to ground plans or master glyphs of magical art.

Once the energy levels increase, visualisations become powerful in their own right, and can often have considerable transformative effect (as opposed to mild therapy, relaxation, reassurance and other relatively trivial ends that seem to play such a great role in most tuition practice and literature). Powerful visualisation usually needs matrices to direct and control the power. Curiously this is not always found in the fundamental visual units of any working such as the scenes, personae, events or transformations that arise but in the inherent pattern, which may be drawn out as a map, or a symbolic or geometric abstract. In this sense the Circle, the Tree of Life, the Three Worlds and other glyphs are *power circuits* just as much as they are metaphysical or psychological conceptual models.

All of the foregoing, however, should be treated with caution; the worst visualisations are often those that plod rigidly through rule-of-thumb steps, stages or grades. Such efforts, and this problem also arises in ritual, are plotted upon the master glyphs, and regarded as inflexible or even sacred. The difference between a pedantic level of working and a creative but disciplined visualisation lives, of course, in inspiration, but it is also found through a meditative understanding of concepts of using imagery for magical transformation, and through skill in relating such imagery to magical patterns.

One of the problems with magical arts is that so many practitioners, some with many years of dedication, fully believe and acclaim that following a rigid formula slavishly will lead to defined results as specified within that very formula. While this attitude may be helpful as a guide in early training, it cannot and does not hold good for the higher modes of consciousness, or the aroused energies of advanced magical visualisation and ritual. Higher consciousness transcends serial patterns and rigid forms; yet it has patterns inherent within itself, and this is a major teaching of ancient traditional cosmology or metaphysics, in which the universe and humanity are conscious reflections of one another, the microcosm of man being a mirror of the macrocosm of divinity. The major glyphs or symbols hold good on many levels of creation or expression, and it is to these symbols that we may look for 'maps' to define our visualisations.

The topology, however, is multidimensional, and never rigid, flat or dogmatically authoritative. Glyphs such as the Fourfold Circle (Circled Cross) or Tree of Life act as templates for comparison rather than as formal final blueprints or dogmatic assertions of direction and relationship. They indicate potential flows or harmonic possibilities of energy, and often have inherent within them many sets of relationship that are totally unknown and inaccessible to serial thinking. Thus they can be used to define a visualisation in map form, but not to lock it into any pre-defined pattern.

The potential and hidden relationships within a master key or glyph are also vitally important in pure meditation or contemplation. In such states, consciousness comprehends relative truths and experiences dynamic transformations beyond exterior form or interior imagery such as is used in visualisation. These higher modes and relationships may, however, be defined and given expression by the process of a symbolic descent, such as working through the Three Worlds or down the Tree of Life. This is traditionally described as a mirroring or echo of the divine act of creation, through which a human entity repeats the metaphysical unfolding or devolution that lead to the exteriorised worlds. If we are able to reach the higher modes of consciousness in the first place, they generate their own imagery for future visualisation if we choose to attune the energies in a visual manner.

Visualisations in Modern Context

The guided visualisations found in modern esoteric practices, be they religious composition of place or magical pathworking or guided scenarios, usually have a written origin. They are, therefore, developments (or devolutions) from the original oral tradition, in which long and often complex tales filled with imagery were spoken, recited or chanted. This incantatory quality, essential to all true poetry even today, is usually absent from modern visualisations.

The problem is not easily solved, for we are accustomed to a literary or more dubious televised ambience for stimulation of our imaginations. The general method in modern magical arts has been to write out a visualisation, and have it read aloud by a skilled visualiser and mediator to the group. This person does not merely *read* the sequence, for he or she must be familiar with every part of it, and actively visualise the images and mediate the forces concerned. This is undoubtedly a demanding requirement, but is an essential skill for advanced magical arts, and hard to equal as an experience in group visualisation and use of imaginative forces.

Even more effective is when the 'reader' is not in fact a reader, but has learned the sequence by heart. The entire procedure is then transformed into an interactive visualisation, for when it is recited in this manner, tiny aspects often change to good effect. On rare occasions, there are major changes, as a result of visionary clues given to the mediator or story-teller from innerworld sources. As a rule, however, such changes must be resisted; it is only through practice and experience that the story-teller learns to accept certain images and present them to the group, while rejecting others. Common sense is still the best rule to apply.

The Examples in this Book

Work with our examples may be undertaken along the lines described above, either in reading aloud from text, or by developing an oral (by heart) presentation of the sequences. One interesting aspect of using written texts in magic is that they are most effective for the individual visualiser when he or she reads them aloud, even though alone. We could enter into sophisticated psychological theories to account for this, but leave it to the experimental spirit of the reader to test for themselves. Once you have read a story aloud several times, you will find that it becomes embedded in the mind more powerfully than if it is read silently.

For those who wish to work from pre-recorded tapes, a complete set of the visualisations published here is available, on stereo cassette, read by the author, with specially composed music. Enquiries should be made to: Sulis Music BCM 3721, London WC1N 3XX.

3

RITUAL

Rituals

There is a common misconception that rituals must be complex
to be powerful; this is not necessarily the case. Before working
with the rituals in this book, a short examination of the state of
modern ritual magic and some of its practices and implications
may be useful.

With a few significant exceptions, the majority of rituals
found in publication are either very recent indeed (written since
the 1950s) or drawn from Victorian literature. The exceptions are
those few ceremonies connected to specific magical systems that
have survived from earlier centuries (such as those of Dr John
Dee or other European Renaissance magi and alchemists), and
of course the diffuse fragments surviving from pagan religion.
As we are working within a Western esoteric tradition, we may
for the moment exclude rituals or ceremonial activities connected to orthodox political religions or to Eastern traditions. In
the context of Eastern rituals, however, it is necessary to state
that certain primal rituals worldwide share common concepts
and symbols; the routes of approach, however, are complex and
widely different through language, culture, tradition and
religious influence.

Advanced magical arts dispense utterly with mystique,
romanticism and pseudo-learning. Thus an advanced ritual may
be quite simple in its form and language, even though it has
complex effects and relationships upon inner levels, and a long
background of development or tradition as a foundation to its
expressed simplicity. The popular illusion that powerful rituals
are complex, lengthy and at times downright incomprehensible
is partly due to our inheritance from experimental Victorian

occultists. We need to see their efforts in the light of the majority of literature of the period, which tended to be prolix, wilfully obscure, and (to the modern reader) somewhat pompous and pedantic. It is not possible to say how such material was regarded in its own time and place; it may be that rituals such as those used in Masonic offshoots and true magical orders such as the Golden Dawn were frightfully modern when compared to the material, or lack of material, of previous societies and of religious services. But there is certainly no law that requires us to copy the rotund style of A. E. Waite,[5] for example, or to indulge certain of the more extreme ravings of McGregor Mathers or Aleister Crowley, where romantic revolution or deliberate sensationalism often mask the profound magical content of the author's work.

Nor is it a stipulation that the modern magician should copy or draw upon the formal language of orthodox religion, though this certainly was the case for many rituals composed in earlier centuries. Some fundamental formulae, however, are common to religion and magical arts worldwide, such as acting 'in the name of', a formula used equally for Christ, Buddha and the earlier pagan deities. We should be aware, therefore, of the difference between hallowed formulae which are part of an established vocabulary of ritual, and dogmatic phraseology borrowed from State religion because of a spurious feeling of 'authority' that might be found therein.

Language in Ritual

Perhaps the most important problem in the language of magical ritual is the temptation to use wilfully obscure material. There is, in fact, a more or less lost art of employing what appears to be total gibberish to steer consciousness into new dimensions; it must be stressed very strongly, however, that this is not identical to hypnotic repetition or similar concepts. The use of proto-words is closely linked to the much-flaunted but little-understood concept of *words of power* and works upon the most fundamental connections between energy, consciousness and verbalising. The true key to John Dee's Enochian material lies in this direction, though no satisfactory interpretation has yet been made of it.

Thus advanced magical arts may employ curious words, chants, vocal tones and other symbolic verbal or uttered units: such units must always be meaningful.[6] In highly developed group work any calls or special tones and words must be understood by *all* members, though it is occasionally known for rituals with people of mixed abilities and background to contain words of power that are fully understood and employed by certain officers but not by all members. In such cases, the context, aim and results of such words must be made clear, as otherwise the group cannot function properly.

There are, of course, a wide range of ritual pattern-making activities. As a general rule, ceremonial magic employs a fusion of various expressed modes of communication: words, music, dance, formal movement, scents, colours, sounds, objective symbols and implements. Thus a very simple ritual text (when considered on paper) may result in a complex and demanding ceremony. Conversely, a lengthy text that appears complex in literary terms may be inadequate in its use of the other aspects of ceremony and pattern-making that are required to fuse a good effective ritual into a transformative event. The worst rites, of course, are those in which endless pages of wordy text are combined with pointless repetitive use of symbols: very often a simple ceremony or a basic meditation can replace an hour or two of replete ritualising.

Innerworld Contact

But where should 'modern' or 'advanced' rituals come from? Clearly they cannot be confined to experimental literature, nor should they be restricted to the published or customary material of the magicians of previous centuries. The entire matter revolves around the major concept of *innerworld contact*. Although there is much disagreement upon this subject between practising magicians, it seems best to combine genuine traditions of magical art (rather than specific books or ritual texts) with new intuitive or *contacted* material.

Innerworld contacts seldom generate totally new schools of magical art (though many self-styled leaders and teachers attempt this unnecessary type of project) but they certainly open out and vitalise aspects of traditional magic and myth that have long been closed to the modern psyche. Furthermore teaching contacts, such as innerworld guides or images of priests, priestesses and magicians, often reveal ways whereby early traditions may be transformed for the future and enabled for present use. If we summarise this process, it is really nothing more or less than one of balance; magic is founded upon very long periods of time and tradition, even though the application of such traditions may result in dynamic and rapid changes. Experienced magicians are very wary indeed of self-declared 'teachers' or new 'revelations', for such material is easily contacted upon the fringes of the imagination, and often benefits no one other than the phantoms or unscrupulous humans who originate it.

Props and Pitfalls

Magical ceremonies from the nineteenth century onwards have a tendency towards complexity. This is evident not merely in the language, sources and intellectual assembly, but in the physical apparatus of any individual, group or ritual. We find complexity in Renaissance magic also, but deriving from rather different concepts. While the apparatus and pattern of Dr John Dee's *Heptarchia Mystica*,[7] for example, was precise and demanding in what would nowadays be termed a scientific manner, and the experiments of other Renaissance magicians drew upon basic planetary correspondences and mythological motifs, the apparatus and pattern of the Golden Dawn ceremonies was greatly concerned with spectacle, and drew heavily upon both Masonic and liturgical sources. But the Golden Dawn, and later derivative societies, also drew and developed material from innerworld contacts, and this is often where the greatest value is found.[8]

Earlier magical ceremonies tended to be more simple, more vital and less equipment-orientated, but we should be careful when making such comparisons. We need to bear in mind that primal ceremonies, or rituals within a pagan culture, are often the manifest aspects of an enduring and sophisticated religion and metaphysics: thus they do not need to rely heavily upon ostentatious display, or overt educational or instructional courses and interpretations. Such display was indeed a feature of classical pagan State religions for both magical and political reasons, but even these, with certain imperial exceptions in late Roman times, were well founded upon organic ancient traditions. Thus the object-orientated mechanical Victorian era generated ceremonies with many appurtenances and redundancies: but in social or historical context these were precisely the means required by the magicians of the day to enter altered states of consciousness. They do not necessarily apply today.

Objects and Power

If we are to develop magical arts for the twenty-first century, the ceremonies should reflect in a very dynamic and concentrated form the requirements of our time.

We have generally discussed the current atrophy of imagination, and our increasing awareness of the sanctity of the land or environmental issues. Both imagination and the sanctity of the land are, and always have been, central subjects in magical art. We would expect such subjects to form a major part of all magical work, from early training to advanced levels. But there are other important concerns that should be reflected in magical arts, and none is more typical of our culture than obsession with objects. We live in a heavily materialised society, in the sense that exterior objects are regarded as essential and desirable in their own right.

It is insufficient to see this as a merely economic matter, the result of rampant capitalism, for it reflects a pattern of collective consciousness that developed slowly over several centuries, then rapidly accelerated with the appearance of new technology and communications media. In magical terms, the acquisition of objects spuriously replaces the realisation of our inner potential. In this curious process of exteriorisation the object (house, car, work-status, television, stereo, video, computer) becomes a visible totem of identity, a declaration of phantom selfhood. Simultaneously we long for such objects not merely to show off to others, but to convince ourselves that we no longer need to look within, for all our needs are met by technological marvels in object form. Nor is this complaint identical to the old

Christianised propaganda that material possessions are bad for the soul or inherently evil; objects are, in truth, nothing more than inherently useful at best or pointlessly trivial at worst. It is our individual and collective obsession that is potentially dangerous, for it leads to enslavement.

In a book of this sort, in which our subject is magical arts, there is no place for a complex discussion of modern society, but we do need to consider how certain potentially crippling social or psychological phenomena may appear within the Circle of Art. Advanced magical ritual should begin to move away from object-orientated ceremonies, and attempt not to rely extensively on technological innovations that replace or inhibit the imagination.

Some very basic examples spring to mind immediately. For example, recorded music can be very effective for visualisation or ritual, but live music performed by a skilled mediator or magician is empowered to a far greater extent. We have the technology readily available to project images within a magical temple, but this would be a complete undermining of the main discipline of visualisation, which consists of image-building within rather than without. Sophisticated lighting is easily achieved by low-price equipment, but magical arts have specific elemental patterns that involve living flames, so candles or oil lamps should not be disposed of.

There is an increasing inclination to regard the Tree of Life as a type of computer, or even to put Kabbalistic 'programs' onto computer: this is a good example of potentially superfluous or even negative exteriorisation of concepts, symbols and polarised sets of relationships that are intended to work specifically in meditation. Our Victorian forebears, with their long lists of pan-cultural multi-lingual straight-jacketed correspondences must, regrettably, bear much of the blame for this tendency. But they, at least, strove individually to search out the details with which they were so obsessed, rather than merely call up simulations by pressing a few keys on an electronic device with no inherent consciousness of its own.

Advanced rituals should not, therefore, use vast arrays of physical objects (as did the Masonic-style nineteenth-century groups) nor should they rely upon technology for matters that belong within the imagination. In other words, we should not need objects to stimulate our inner energies through association. Advanced magical arts reverse this process, and the inner energies sanctify or endow the chosen objects with required properties. This is a very ancient magical concept indeed, and needs to be kept firmly in mind for practical work.

During this short discussion, we have moved conceptually from the Lunar World (which includes our outer or physical body, thoughts and emotions) towards the Solar World: suddenly we have left objects behind as stimuli or associative symbols, but we may now return to them as vessels of power. This concept is found in the UnderWorld traditions worldwide, in which magical objects are hidden within the depths of the earth, and have to be claimed, achieved or exchanged for human benefit. The Grail is the great spiritual vessel of the UnderWorld in Western tradition, but the other treasures of Merlin are also of considerable importance. This UnderWorld tradition reflects exactly the OverWorld or Solar World in which a redeeming or transforming spiritual influence changes outer conditions: these conditions may be the human 'lower' self or Lunar consciousness and body; they may also be objects or locations within the land or planet.

Traditionally we are taught that transformative energies may flow through *Gates* or metaphysical archetypes or matrices, either into the human body/consciousness or directly (via the UnderWorld) into the material world, and empower locations, crystals, plants or even artificial structures. Various theories account for this material effect, ranging from the old Elemental and Planetary influences to geomagnetic and bio-electrical fields; however we seek to rationalise or detail the matter, it involves force flowing into form and becoming inherent within that form (see Figure 5). The direct enhancement of form by force, that of material objects, is nowadays a neglected aspect of magical work.[9]

It is often assumed, for example, that an object (such as a chalice, wand, sword or shield used in ceremonial magic) becomes charged or loaded with energy in the same way that an electrical battery may be charged: this is not entirely the case, though temporary vitalisation of objects can easily be achieved by group working. It is worth pursuing this subject in some detail, as it is crucial to ritual work in general, and of increasing importance in developing magical arts.

Figure 5.   The OverWorld and UnderWorld Tree of Life.

The unified Tree of the UnderWorld shows the descending levels of the UnderWorld Initiation.

*   While the upper Tree is the usual meditational key employed in Western occultism, it is the Reflected Tree that enables us to energise the structure within our own body/psychic complex.*

Reflected Tree
10: The Physical Body.
7– 8–9: Passing Within: experiencing the individual psychic-energetic entity.
4 –5– 6: Experiencing the Powers of Giving (Sphere 4) and Taking (5) which merge and transform into the Fruit of Light (6).
2–3–1: Experiencing the Universal nature of Consciousness.

In meditation this sequence is operated by visualising a descent through the physical body to an inner centre or source. As suggested by our diagram it is harmonically equivalent to the standard use of the Tree of Life in 'rising through the planes' or ascending from level to level in visualisation.

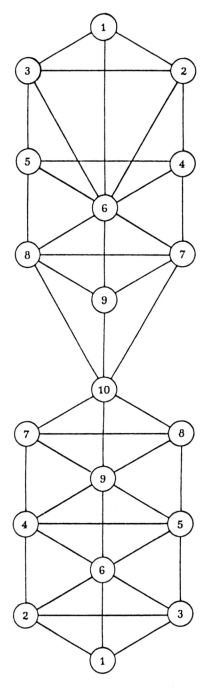

Consecrated Objects

A consecrated object has a certain force *inherent within it*. This force does not drain away, and does not need to be habitually renewed or conditioned or recharged: further 'charge' may indeed be given through ceremony or group vital energies, but the spiritual force has permanently empowered the physical form. This is a typical example of a Solar or, more rarely, Stellar magical operation, in which the higher faculties of consciousness and energy re-attune a normally mundane object to the resonance of the higher worlds. A consecrated object, in this sense, becomes not merely a vessel in the sense of a bottle or container, but an actual variant or harmonic presentation of a higher force. The Four Implements of ritual magic are the most widely known examples of this, for they reflect through their outer form certain inner or perpetual truths regarding the nature of Being and the forces of origination, creation, formation and expression.

This convenient 'vertical' division of levels of manifestation or reflection is the Spindle around which rotates the Fourfold Cycle, commencing as divine powers or Life, Light, Love and Law, and appearing as the Elements of Air, Fire, Water and Earth in the outer worlds (see Figure 6). A consecrated implement is present in all worlds, Lunar, Solar and Stellar, active or potentially active through all four phases of manifestation or reflection (expression, formation, creation and origination) and serves to fuse the concepts and energies of the Powers (Life, Light, Love and Law) with those of the Four Elements. The implements are not, as is often suggested, tools for control of the Elements or of entities, but a cycle of forms embodying forces. These forms incorporate all harmonic levels or worlds in which their force appears and operates. This type of connective use of concepts is very important indeed in magic, and is developed extensively through meditation, visualisation and ritual pattern-making. It need hardly be said that such an empowering does not come from wishful thinking, association, conditioning or force of will on the part of a human: it is activated in two possible ways.

The first is the ancient and nowadays little-used technique of seeking transformation within the UnderWorld: the initiate who has undergone the UnderWorld experience brings back, so to

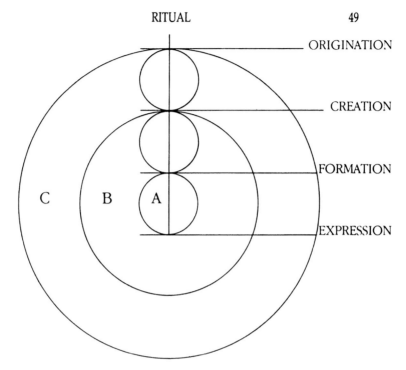

Figure 6   The Three Worlds and the Fourfold Reflection

speak, the hallowed objects, which become unified with his or her physical symbols of sword, rod, cup or shield.

The second way is best-known in standard magico-religious technique: the magician applies to higher forces and entities for a blessing, act of grace, or harmonious co-operation in the consecration of an object. The principle behind this is identical in every way to the operation of any successful ritual: consciousness must become active in higher dimensions, and form a through line or set of reflections by which energy is communicated into the physical world. This is exactly why magical tradition teaches the concept of Worlds and Spheres, not as a dogmatic assertion of metaphysical reality, but as a method of attuning consciousness and energies through imaginal matrices and cosmological concepts.

If we expand our consciousness into the Stellar World, the subsequent reflections or lower worlds are included and dissolved (see Figure 1) in universal Wisdom, Understanding and spiritual Being. Paradoxically this is exactly why the UnderWorld magical techniques are so powerful, for the magician finds the stellar powers within the planet, or the spiritual force inherent within matter. It need hardly be said that our physical bodies are, of course, such matter.

4

MEDIATION

Mediation is a major feature of advanced magical arts; as a technique it is crucial to most practical operations, and as a spiritual undertaking it fulfils a number of the dedications of service that are found in all traditions of enlightenment. The practice of mediation may be considered and conducted in two ways: that of personae or images, and that of specific power, consciousness or energies. Each of these methods or interpretations is readily interchangeable with the other, but as a rule they are put into practice individually due to the considerable effort required to build the necessary thought-forms, images or inner skills to enable either kind of function. There are both advantages and disadvantages to each method or conceptual approach; we should initially consider them separately even though they ultimately represent a single inner process of mediation of energy from originative states beyond definition or form. For mediation to develop and to become manifest as outer results, discipline, form and clear concepts are essential.

Telesmatic Images or Personae

This first approach to mediation is the best-known, and certainly the most frequently employed in general magical work. It also has a long tradition reaching back for millennia, and bridges many religions, cultures, schools of esoteric development, and the work of individual adepts. *Mediation* of images, personae or god-forms is still confused, even in well-established magical groups, with *mediumship*. Such confusion usually arises because of the employment of innerworld personae and images in mediation, for superficially a similar process is found in mediumship. The two psychic events or abilities are not identical, however, and in a strict technical sense they are not even related.

Mediumship is an atavistic talent, still known today, which was widely used in ancient religions, temple rituals, and in the sub-strata of general magic in the pagan and early Christian world. It enjoyed a considerable revival in the nineteenth century and still exists as a fairly minor Christian sub-cult or as a commercial activity deriving from the Victorian enthusiasm for 'spiritualism'. Mediumship is also found worldwide in the practices of primitive peoples, though we should be cautious in such definitions, as many apparently primitive races employ very sophisticated magical arts hand in hand with crude superstitions and debased practices. We should add that classical pagan practices included both mediumship and mediation, particularly in the higher levels of working, and the inner instructions of the Mysteries.

The important difference between mediation and mediumship, as has often been described, is that a medium is passive and generally unaware of that which he or she transfers, while a mediator is active and in a state of heightened consciousness and amplified awareness without any loss of individuality. A medium may even be rendered unconscious and apparently be replaced by another entity that uses the body and communicative apparatus in a parasitic manner. This type of displacement does not occur in mediation, as both the intent of the mediator and the methods required to put that intent into operation preclude such replacement.

A mediator attunes his or herself to specific concepts, symbols, realms or dimensions of consciousness (Worlds). This is accomplished through intense meditation, visualisation and concentration, amplified by ritual pattern-making. Furthermore a skilled mediator is usually steeped in the specific tradition that he or she seeks to enliven by mediation of a specific telesmatic image or innerworld entity. A medium may, at best, be able to contact a limited number of pre-defined personae who act as mentors or guides by displacing or suppressing the customary personality or identity. Apart from such major differences in technique and actual operation, there is a significant difference between mediation and mediumship in quality, intensity of power, and the type of entity contacted.

A skilled mediator may work with any chosen entity or telesmatic image; this open range of potential is quite unknown in mediumship, which seems to be confined to deceased relatives, dedicated 'spirit guides' and exotic personae such as Chinese masters, Red Indians and other products of romantic notions still redolent of Victorian sentiment. While mediumship relates relatively trivial but often reassuring communications, and cannot reach a higher level unless, as was the ancient practice, attuned to a specific Mystery, mediation deals with transmission of power through specific entities, images or personae.

In mediation the entities or personae contacted are occasionally defined as innerworld teachers, but more frequently they are beings described in myth, legend, mystical psychology and magical or religious traditions. This is a very important definition indeed, for there is little point in developing higher modes of consciousness and skill in magical arts merely to gossip with the phantoms of deceased relatives: indeed, such superficial temporary (time-bound) personae do not exist in the higher worlds or modes of consciousness, for they are properties of the psyche still close to the outer consensual world. They are quite different, for example, to the advisory and message-carrying *daemones* of medieval tradition (as found in the Merlin cosmology described by Geoffrey of Monmouth, and in various source texts from classical times), which dwell in the sub-lunar realm and are made pure through the interaction between themselves, humanity and divinity.

The entities contacted in mediation may wear a number of different personae, for personae are only *masks*. This truth is typified in a number of myths in which a central character changes identity or even gender, for the spiritual individuality is not confined to any temporary personality or characteristic. This illusory confinement is of course the great flaw in so-called spiritualism, for advanced consciousness does not remain upon the realms of material reflection and idle trivia. Thus a mediator may bring through the specific consciousness of an innerworld master, but this could legitimately be regarded as a waste of time and energy, for such teachers are more easily contacted through regular effort in individual meditation and visualisation, requiring neither mediation or crude mediumship.

What is the central purpose of mediation, therefore? It is generally employed to give *form* to *force*. High levels of power are defined and shaped through images, and the images (entities, personae, telesmata and god- or goddess-forms) are attuned to the psyche of the mediator. The physical body then acts as a transmitter of energies modulated to relate to the magical circle and eventually to the outer world. Mediation is an act of bridging dimensions or states of consciousness and energy, not of replacing one ephemeral personality with another. A mediator may work with images such as mythical heroes, priests or priestesses, gods and goddesses. In an orthodox religious context (though such practices are generally forbidden) a mediator might work with saints, angels, teachers and similar bridging images. The 'reality' of such entities is irrelevant, for they are no more or less real than our outer selves. The major art of mediation, however, involves highly defined and specialist god- and goddess-forms, the telesmatic images of enduring magical and mystical practices.

Telesmatic images are employed to give shape and direction to powerful forces that might otherwise dissipate or even become potentially dangerous upon a human level of consciousness; the mediator assumes or takes upon his or herself the pre-defined image, and thus channels the forces inherent within them, forces which are drawn from higher modes or worlds into which the images act as keys or matrices.

Direct Mediation

It is also possible to mediate power directly, without the extensive use of telesmatic images, and without the assumption or 'bringing through' of entities or personae. Direct mediation may have some advantages for modern magical work, particularly if the developing magician or group seek to bypass well-established lines of imagery within the Western traditions, and attempt to generate a new vocabulary of their own.

Such efforts are not by any means unknown, the best-documented being the *Heptarchia Mystica* of Dr John Dee,[7] the Elizabethan adept. Although Dee used a very high religious tone and true Christian foundation for all his work, the *Heptarchia* seems to be a self-contained and powerful magical system communicted directly by innerworld entities, through the seership of Edward Kelly. Its relationship to orthodox angelology and Kabbalah is superseded by unusual and individual contents, entities and symbols. Other attempts at independent magical systems also exist, many unpublished and generally unavailable in literature, though such systems may be learnt through meditation and inner plane contact in the time-hallowed manner of magical education. We should stress, however, that the purpose of mediation is not to build up alternative magical systems of symbolism. It is first and foremost to mediate, bridge, bring through, and extend power or consciousness between the various worlds, planes, dimensions and states of being.

From the early medieval period the main glyph for both mediation and magical education has been the Tree of Life, which is primarily but by no means exclusively a Kabbalistic apparatus. The mathematical Tree of Life from Jewish and Arabic sources seems to be an amalgam of mathematical metaphysics, such as the Platonic solids, with the fundamental and widespread concepts of a world-tree, well defined in European pagan religion and philosophy before the mathematical variant appeared. The Tree of Life is a major tuitional and operational glyph that divides and yet relates macrocosmic and microcosmic energies and entities; this relationship is shown as levels or Worlds, and as structures of polarity (the pair, the triad, the quaternity and so forth). It is particularly concerned with *harmonic* relationships, whereby power from one level or state reappears harmonically or with a mathematical or conceptual affiliation upon another level. This harmonic similarity is a fundamental concept in practical magic.

Both the Tree of Life, the Spiral of Worlds and the Fourfold Circle may be used as maps for direct mediation of power. Thus in the simplest sense, we might attune to the Element of Air, at the Eastern Quarter of the Circle. Without using anthropomorphic or telesmatic images, we summon the power of Air and *mediate* this power through into the circle. Such mediation may be on a very narrow individual scale, or it may be broadly defined by the position of officers during a ceremony, for the officer of the East will mediate the power of Air as an undertone or foundation to any specific image that he or she also mediates within the structure of the ritual.

On the Tree of Life, it is possible to mediate the energy of a Sphere in a relatively 'pure' form, though this may become increasingly difficult with the supernal and higher spheres without the interface of telesmatic images to adapt and indeed summon the energies concerned. Thus we might seek to mediate the power of the fifth Sphere, or Severity. This catabolic individual collective and cosmic force is often represented by the planetary image and god-form of Mars, the classical god of war. More subtly it is represented upon deeper levels by the goddesses of taking, such as the Celtic Morrigan or the Etruscan Minerva.

But if we mediate the energies *direct* without the telesmatic anthropomorphic images, this must be achieved through long discipline in meditation and concentration. Without the imaginal form to retain consciousness and energy, such an operation depends solely upon a fusion of the lower faculties of concentration with the highest faculties of intuition and spiritual intent. In simpler terms, merely thinking about the power does nothing; we have to become a vessel for it, and actively bridge it through to the magical circle or to the outer world.

The usual method is to begin at the human level of the sphere or energy required, and to elevate or ascend the consciousness into the higher worlds, reaching to transpersonal levels and holding the power steady as each new level is achieved. The power is brought through by the mediator, and descended or modulated by other officers within the matrix of the ceremony. The primary mediator or mediators remain constantly attuned to the original world, archetype or level of power required by them, confident that their fellow group members will undertake the modulation and structuring. There is both an organic and a mechanical analogy that may be drawn here, for component parts in any organism, or mechanism, work together to make the whole entity operative, yet they have individual identity and functions in their own right.

Mediation and the Higher Self

In well-publicised modern systems of magic, such as the comprehensive Golden Dawn papers, the subject of the *Higher Self* or *Holy Guardian Angel* occasionally appears. Knowledge of the Holy Guardian Angel is one of the highest aims of many theosophic and theurgic ceremonies; this major concept is drawn from Jewish mysticism, Gnosticism, and can be traced back in varying forms through the philosophy of Plato to the ancient Mysteries. It is closely related to the dialectic of *Eros* and *Agape* as found in Platonic and primal Christian teachings, yet has been heavily coloured by orthodox Judaeo-Christian religion.[10] The concept of Knowledge of the Holy Guardian Angel or Higher Self and the magical or mystical techniques associated with such knowledge are found worldwide in various guises, and are integral to human spiritual traditions.[11]

In a Western literary context the nature of the Higher Self or Guardian Angel is sometimes confused, and most especially in connection with the major magical art of *mediation*. We have already discussed some aspects of mediation, in which an archetype or apparently self-determining entity is attuned to the outer or collective world through the consciousness of a skilled mediator. This is a very specific, ancient, well-established and defined magical art, unconnected to spiritualism or that thinly disguised contemporary revival of spiritualism known as 'channelling'. In this last sense, the term *guardian angel* is rather unfortunate, for it has many sentimental Victorian undertones and spiritualist connotations.

The Higher Self is that transpersonal and ultimately trans-human spiritual consciousness that may be realised through specific disciplines, or on occasions through unusual circumstances. Magical ceremonies fuse unusual circumstances with specific disciplines to achieve various ends, including realisation of the Higher Self.

Before proceeding further with our discussion of mediation archetypes and the Higher Self, we should bear in mind the strong conditioning influence of terminology. In a prophetic or mystical sense, we can state that there is no such entity as the Higher Self, there is only Divinity, the Absolute. But in many specific traditions the term 'Higher Self' or a similar definition is used to describe an altered state of consciousness that transcends personality and communes with the eternal. This spiritual state is taught as a higher spiral or octave of the ego, into which the ego is absorbed. We shall return to this discussion in the context of technical magical operations shortly.

The language and structure of symbols used within any

system of inner development will pre-condition or mould any account or description of that tradition's effect and results. The terms employed vary considerably, but are unified by certain core concepts that they hold in common. This does not imply that they may all be reduced to one basic system, or that the aims and results of different religious, metaphysical, magical or mystical schools are identical.

We could say, for example, that divinity is found *within*, a major approach particularly developed in both Eastern and Western esoteric disciplines. Alternatively the primal Under-World tradition, found in varying forms worldwide, brings a chthonic and environmental consideration into the technique, wherein movement of consciousness and energy *inwards* becomes movement *downwards* and spiritual energy is found within the earth . . . within the land or planet itself. This tradition has an echo in the Kabbalistic assertion that both Crown and King-dom (Spirit and Matter, or divinity and the consensual world) world) are inherent within one another. Thus by *reflection* the UnderWorld or chthonic magical arts and initiations provide a Shortened Way to spiritual transformation. Movement inwards and downwards equates, metaphysically and paradoxically, to movement upwards: this 'upwards' movement being the linear manner in which we are often conditioned to define altered or increased consciousness, and of course to relate to divinity in orthodox religions.

Both the UnderWorld and the OverWorld contain the universe, for they are within one another. Each conceptual model has its problems: the OverWorld, particularly as known in orthodox and political religion, tends to place spiritual truth or divinity at a very great remove from humanity, often with a hierarchical priesthood conveniently located on earth as the sole true source of mediation of divine will. In esoteric arts this problem becomes modified and reappears as a type of spiritual superiority or 'top-heavy' tendency in which the higher worlds or modes of consciousness are sought as ends in themselves at the expense of the lower. Such divisive concepts are limiting and deluding in the pursuit of true spiritual realisation or communion with the Absolute.

The UnderWorld, a much-neglected tradition of considerable power, does away with superior and divisive concepts altogether, but is not without psychic risks for the untrained or unwary traveller. It offers great energy and potency, often without instruction or support; it is an experience rather than a philosophy or a religion. We might be tempted to think that a fusion of the two conceptual models, Over and Under Worlds, could provide an answer to the problem, but in practice this simplistic solution is difficult to realise.

Magical systems, still emerging today from centuries of confusion and neglect, contain fragments of all of the foregoing conceptual viewpoints and methods of approach to Truth. Sometimes they include vast edifices of symbolism and ceremony, but more often they comprise suggestive insights and partial keys to matters which are only elucidated inwardly through long effort and discipline. Once again we are forced to the conclusion that the much-vaunted *complete system of magic*, no matter what its original source, is either a fraud or a delusion: completeness (which is a spurious desire) is found within, in the realisation of truth, rather than upon a printed page or through membership of a group, training class or magical society.

When we discuss the Higher Self, therefore, we are not suggesting a super-being that floats just above the human head, or hides in a dimension usually inaccessible and emits lower selves like spores into the material world (this last being a favourite pseudo-rationalisation in the nineteenth century). The Higher Self begins, for us, as a working definition; it helps us to give a temporary and disposable form to a universal spiritual force transcending language and definition. We partake of that force, yet paradoxically we feel ourselves to be separated from it. The concept of the Higher Self is, in itself, a type of telesmatic image that can be employed in mediation, but it does not usually take an archetypical visual form. We shall return to this subject of relationship between the Higher Self and telesmata shortly.

In esoteric instruction the Higher Self or Holy Guardian Angel is indicated upon the basic Tree of Life by Spheres 6 and 1, and by the path between them, connecting the Solar and Stellar Worlds. This corresponds, in terms of the Axis Mundi and basic cosmology, to the tarot trump of The Star. There are various refinements of theory regarding the spiritual entity, including some highly intellectual systems which suggest that many 'personalities' in our outer world are emitted by a single over-soul or transcendent entity. In magical work there is a tendency to bypass such complexities and aim for direct experience. There can be little doubt that certain disciplines, magical arts and rituals lead to an expansion and transformation of consciousness in which the regular personality is subsumed into a higher order or entity. In advanced mystical and magical arts, the higher entity or higher octaves or consciousness descend into the lower even as the lower ascends, and the two apparently separate forms are unified.

This transformation is traditionally defined through three different stages, and despite varieties of technical description, we may summarise these (with reference to the Tree of Life or Spiral of Worlds) as follows.

First Stage

Human personal and collective consciousness; the Lunar World; Spheres 10, 9, 8, 7 and 6 upon the Tree of Life. This is the self, the ego of materialist psychology, and the 'Lower Self'. But we must be very cautious indeed that these definitions of higher and lower do not become value judgements: they are merely terms of reference and not statements of quality or relative inferiority or superiority. The UnderWorld tradition demonstrates very clearly that the so-called *lower* self and lower worlds are an immense source of spiritual enlightenment and declaration of divine presence.

The first stage, spiral or *World* of energies is founded upon the Lunar Sphere, and a circle with its centre upon the Foundation encompasses the body or manifest elements, the mind, the emotions, and includes transcendent consciousness. Such simple geometry upon a well-proportioned Tree of Life gives many insights in meditation, visualisation and ritual pattern-making. The Lunar World thresholds or limits are clearly defined by the planetary forces of Earth, Moon, Mercury, Venus and the Sun in astrology, mythology and magical arts. Many of the telesmatic images used in magic relate to these spheres, and are frequently the subject of mediation in ritual work. (See Figure 3.)

The Tree of Life refines the concepts of Spheres and Planets by connecting Paths, often represented by tarot trumps in modern magical systems. At its nadir the Lunar World includes the collective organic and mineral consciousness, and touches upon the UnderWorld. At its zenith it includes solar consciousness, in which awareness transcends human personality and reaches into spiritual dimensions. It is essential to realise and admit that the majority of spiritual experiences reach only to this zenith, and that many of the higher modes of consciousness attained in ritual or meditation are clearly symbolised by Paths which approach this solar zenith of the Lunar World. Thus Knowledge of the Higher Self (or Guardian Angel) is at first defined by a fusion of solar and lunar energies, symbolised by the tarot trump The Sun, and by other emblems of harmonious, balanced, enlightened, and transformed consciousness/energy.

In human terms this is traditionally taught as the *Arousal of the Inner Fire*, a discipline in which the direction of life energies (normally attuned to sexual gratification) is reversed. The Inner Fire is nothing less than our 'sexual energy' aspiring (breathing or rising) towards a spiritual arousal. The Lunar Sphere or Foundation of the Tree of Life is the home of such energies: they may flow outwards to the Kingdom, or move inwards and arise towards the Sphere of Beauty and Harmony, symbolised by the Sun. Ultimately the polarised flow of energy is balanced, but in magical training it takes most of our effort to maintain an inward direction rather than outward conditioning.

Thus far we have summarised the first stage of knowledge of the Higher Self, in which an experience is gained that confirms higher consciousness in an undeniable manner. This is the so-called 'enlightenment' which features so strongly in many initiatory and Eastern cult systems, but it is not necessarily a permanent stage or ability, and that which is gained, even through effort and discipline, may be easily lost.

The Solar World, and specifically the 6th Sphere of Harmony and Beauty, symbolised by the physical sun, is the dwelling or condition of Being associated with the Redeemer. This is not confined as a concept to Christian or even Messianic tradition, for it includes pagan or non-Christian redeemers, Sons of Light, Saints, and spiritual mediators and mentors. In classical myth we find the solar heroes and deities in this sphere: in short all images, forms, expressions or entities of Harmony, Light, Balance or Enlightenment are uttered forth from this transcendent consciousness. Just as the sun is at the centre of the solar system, so is the spiritual Solar Being at the centre of the Solar World.

Upon the Tree of Life we have a visual key to the technical operation in which *aspiration* may be fuelled by emotion (Sphere 7, Venus, Victory) or clarified and amplified through the intellect (Sphere 8, Mercury, Glory). Ideally these two pivots of ·consciousness merge together; upon such a fusion central or foundational energies arise, elevating awareness, and giving rise to illumination.

In religious practices an altered state of consciousness is often gained through devotion to a great harmonising influence, Redeemer, Saviour or Enlightened One; Christ and Buddha are typical examples, while the pagan world had both male and female images that inspired devotion and aspiration. In the Western world today the feminine aspect is broadly covered by the Catholic image of the Virgin, which has absorbed all other goddesses. One of the major projects of advanced magical arts today is to reinstate feminine forms in ceremonial work; such a reinstatement is a far cry from popular 'paganism' or 'goddess revival' as most of these movements are still in a very early and often juvenile or imbalanced state. As is often the case with magical arts, the ferment will not settle until one or two generations have passed.

Magical arts often employ images from early or neglected traditions and religions, not through wilful obscurity, but because such images may (with careful use) lead to rapid highly energised results. In other words the telesmatic images of magico-religious traditions may bypass the clogged and frequently corrupted routes of political religion. This problem is found particularly in the context of Christianity, the most politicised and propagandised of all world religions.

Second Stage

Spiritual transpersonal consciousness; the Solar World; Spheres 6, 5, 4, 7, 8, and 9; and the Bridge across the Abyss (Known as *Daath* in Hebrew mysticism). This *World* is centred upon the 6th Sphere, known as Beauty or Harmony. Its nadir is the Foundation or Moon, and its zenith is the Bridge across the Abyss that separates Solar from Stellar reality, or our sun from other stars. Thus a circle with its centre as Sphere 6, when drawn upon the Tree of Life, encompasses the Spheres or defining energies of Venus, Luna, Mercury, Mars and Jupiter; or Victory, Foundation, Glory, Severity and Mercy.

This second stage corresponds in many ways to the traditional concept of 'conversation with' the Guardian Angel or Higher Self. That which was at first a zenith experience may, through constant attention and discipline, become central to the consciousness. This is the permanent transformation of the heart, in which spiritual and transpersonal truths emerge from the Inner Fire, and replace biological and personal interests or conditions. There is no ridiculous concept of abandoning the body or leaving 'unclean' things behind: the Lunar World turns through a spiral or octave, and *becomes* the Solar World. This is a permanent state of enlightenment beyond personality, but the personality is included within it through the thoughts, emotions and foundational energies of Spheres 8, 7 and 9. The Tree of Life, it should be remembered, does not provide a rigid rule-of-thumb guide or methodology; it gives us a harmonic set of concepts that merge into one another, and these help us to define certain changes of consciousness and energy which might otherwise have no vocabulary, or might become so clogged with technical definition that the reality be lost altogether.

While Stage One (experience of the Lunar World) gives flashes of illumination and enlightenment, Stage Two (experience of the Solar World) is traditionally said to admit the initiate to the Convocation of Light. This convocation is a *state of consciousness*, though it is frequently represented in visual terms as a place or inner dimension with landscape, features, people and other attributes. The Abbey, College, Castle and Observatory motifs found in various visualisations are typical of such structures, but it must be stressed that building the outer form as an imaginative exercise does not guarantee admission to the convocation. There is only an arbitrary difference, in magical concept, between *state, place, and plane or dimension*. As we have repeatedly emphasised, the human imagination works through forms, but the forms embody forces.

The Convocation of Light, sometimes equated with the Universal Mind or the Knower, is where all harmonically related and enlightened consciousness merges. It is not a cosy ideal or heavenly condition, but a property of consciousness and energy that occurs only through awakening and union with the Higher

Self. Paradoxically such union, the apparent zenith of individuality, leads to a convocation or harmonic intersection with many other entities. Thus a universal mind is touched, a condition in which knowledge is attained direct, and in which many individual minds may join together. This is not, of course the sole property of the universal mind, but it describes an experience regularly defined by magical arts and other esoteric disciplines.

The Convocation of Light is at the centre of the Solar World; in old-fashioned terms we might say that it is the light of illuminated souls, giving birth to the fire of the sun. The energies of the convocation are reflected through the Lunar World, which gives them form. This brings us back to the visual constructs used in specific magical arts, many of which are featured in our examples of visualisation. We must also remember that *all* forms are defined in the Lunar World, and not fall into the trap of separating the consensual outer world from that of our imagination.

The solar enlightenment, or Convocation of Light, should not be confused with collective or ancestral consciousness, which is found in the Lunar World and UnderWorld. It is, however, a higher octave of that same collective, and as such unknown to materialist psychology.

The Paths found within the Solar World are of particular importance for the higher or more drastic initiations in magic: they involve transformations which are deep and permanent, and may not be easily rescinded or regressed. Many of the most potent telesmatic images derive from this World, and may only be successfully energised by the magician who has some true Knowledge or enlightenment.

The zenith, which is both the Abyss and its Crossing, is that moment of truth in which stellar awareness, or universal mind, is first attained. It crosses the Abyss of time and space, and reaches into realms and modes of consciousness hardly touched by humanity, though accessible to us through various methods of transformation and enlightenment.

The Third Stage

The last transformation or stage of Knowledge involves crossing the Abyss and merging consciousness with the supernal

Spheres, the Stellar World. On the Tree of Life we find Spheres 1, 2, and 3, or Crown, Wisdom and Understanding. These have further attributes of Uranus, Neptune and Saturn, or *Primum Mobile*, Zodiac and Saturn. The universal Being, Outgoing and Ingoing principles (Spirit, Father and Mother). A further step is known, which leads into the Void, known in Kabbalah as the *Ain Soph*. This non-state is acknowledged by the phrase *Peace is a Secret Unknown* in our examples of ritual or visualisation.

The Higher Self and Telesmatic Images

If we examine primitive magical arts, we find that they appear to operate upon an ancestral and elemental level; the concept of a transpersonal reality is present but often unrealised. It appears mainly as an ancestral stream of awareness, within which spiritual truth is found through the collective wisdom of many forebears. This perspective is refined by the appearance of specific heroes and sacred kings, who in time lead to the concept of a universal Redeemer or Redeeming Power. But we should not be misled by the implication of evolution in this picture, for serial time and linear development play little or no part upon the deeper levels of consciousness. The presence of a universal Saviour or Redeemer (whose name changes from age to age and world to world) cuts across illusions of time, space and events. We cannot hold to the notion of ignorant ancestors struggling towards enlightenment, particularly as magical experience reveals that much enlightenment is found through communion with these same ancestors.

A restatement of this ancestral theory is found in the definition of the unconscious made by C. G. Jung,[12] but we must be extremely cautious in equating Jung's concepts with those of traditional magical and spiritual psychology. Although he plundered many ancient systems from both East and West extensively for terminology, theories and techniques, Jung also altered many concepts. Thus terms and theories that appear superficially to be held in common with Western or Eastern esoteric psychologies by Jung and the later Jungians, are often found to be radically different on closer examination. There has been a massive period of trite unquestioning lip-service to psychology, particularly that of Jung, by modern magical, astrological and esoteric writers and researchers, often without any deeply considered examination of the esoteric traditions in their own right.

Modern psychology deals effectively with one level or spiral of consciousness, which we have defined as the Lunar World; it is that area of the Tree of Life that includes the body, vital energies, thoughts and emotions, with a zenith or potentially transpersonal area that emanates all of the foregoing. These were symbolised in traditional astrology by Earth, Moon, Mercury, Venus and the Sun. As we have suggested above, there are two higher spirals or Worlds, the Solar and the Stellar World shown upon the Axis Mundi or Tree of Life.

All three Worlds are modified within human perception and presented as archetypes, forms or images. Such forms may be abstract or geometric philosophical entities, such as those of Plato and of the mathematical schools of mystical symbolism, or they may appear as anthropomorphic and theriomorphic beings as in all world religions and wisdom traditions, legends, myths and esoteric instruction or training. Much confusion arises from nineteenth- and twentieth-century attempts to systematise archetypes or images, even though simple harmonic world-views and cosmologies are well known in Western literature from the earliest periods.

For practical purposes we may use the Tree of Life and the ubiquitous tarot to demonstrate associations between the Higher Self or spiritual entity and the forms or telesmatic images. While there are complex systems known from nineteenth-century occultism these have no inherent authority or organic living tradition to support them. They are, in fact, the remarkable efforts of occultists in Britain and France to rational-ise their confused inheritance of Masonry, pan-cultural theoso-phy, orthodox religion, Hebrew mysticism, Renaissance humanism and European mythology. Whatever the sources, they were further complicated by material from innerworld sources, and in many cases this is the most valuable of all. Without this nineteenth- and early twentieth-century revival, which forms a transitional literature rather than a definitive or authoritative source, the present development of esoteric arts and sciences might not have arisen.

But to gain further insights, we need to dispose of much of the assembled rationalised material, particularly where it was incorporated from oriental traditions without any deep experience of those traditions as a living force. Many of the complexities of cosmology, psychology, angelology, elemental beings and so forth that abound in occult literature are simply irrelevant. We may work successfully with a basic Tree of Life, the Fourfold Circle or Wheel of Life, and related cosmology and psychology. A very clear and well-defined system, including tarot trump images and elemental patterns, is found as early as the *Vita Merlini* set into Latin from oral bardic tradition in Britain by Geoffrey of Monmouth (*c*. 1150). This vision of creation, balanced by an apocalyptic vision in the *Prophecies of Merlin* set into Latin by the same writer a few years earlier, pre-dates the first known tarot cards in Renaissance Italy by three centuries, yet contains clear descriptions and definitions of tarot relating to cosmology and psychology.[13]

Clearly our Victorian occultists missed these important texts, or failed to grasp their significance, which is that they indicate magical oral traditions preserved in story-telling or visionary form well into the medieval period. Far from being obscurities, the Merlin texts stand out as crystal-clear systems of symbology when compared to those of Victorian intellectual occultism that still dominate modern literature. If we are to generate advanced magical arts, we should always seek a combination of clarity and tradition, rather than intellectualise our way into such complex thickets of attributes and correspondences that we can no longer see the original purpose of the exercise.

Early tarot traditions involved an elemental cosmology and magical psychology, preserved by bards or poets, and much later formalised as images upon card. It was this tradition that was absorbed and regenerated by the Renaissance, with the *Triumphs* of the poet Petrarch (using traditional emblems and images) giving birth to the word *trumps*. And it is this primal tradition that we can employ to define trumps or Paths upon the Tree of Life or Axis Mundi, realising that many variant forms also exist.

Our main purpose in this chapter is to examine the potential relationship between the Higher Self and telesmatic images used in magical visualisation and ceremony. Before we consider tarot as a symbolic tool in this context, we can refer first to the well-established concept that the Tree of Life consists of a holism of Worlds, emanated from unified Being. In Kabbalah there are four such worlds, defined as Origination, Creation, Formation and Expression. These may also be defined as the Stellar, Solar and Lunar Worlds of the Axis Mundi, the basic spiralling vision or Tree that underpins Western esoteric symbolism. The affiliations are as follows:

Stellar World	Origination/Creation
Solar World	Creation/Formation
Lunar World	Formation/Expression

Upon the Tree of Life (Figure 7) we find that the origination of the Crown or 1st Sphere is reflected through the creation of Beauty or the 6th Sphere, which in turn is given formation by the Foundation or 9th Sphere, to be expressed as the Kingdom, outer world or 10th Sphere. The Axis Mundi or Middle Pillar shows the Three Worlds clearly; we could add a typical Kabbalistic sophistication at this point and suggest that each of the three Axis Mundi Paths (between 10/9/6/1) may be shown as a complete Tree of Life. Thus we would have Lunar, Solar and Stellar Trees. These correspond to the tarot trumps of Moon, Sun and Star, with thresholds of the Wheel of Fortune, Justice and Judgement. Thus we have the simple but effective cosmology of the Three Worlds and the Three Wheels. Once the trumps of the Axis Mundi are recognised, the remaining trumps fall into a spiralling pattern relating to each of the Three Worlds.

Archetypes, Forms and Images

The archetypes, forms and images may be seen in three ways:

1. Lunar Cycle: aspects of personality or archetypes known within the individual and collective consciousness. But magical psychology includes other orders of being, such as Elementals, which also appear in this cycle.
2. Solar Cycle: aspects of transpersonal awareness, or archetypes of a creative and spiritual consciousness.
3. Stellar Cycle: Universal archetypes or forms which act as matrices for originative power, defining and moulding its reflection through to expression.

In tarot we have twenty-two trump images revealing a changing pattern of archetypes rotating around the Axis Mundi

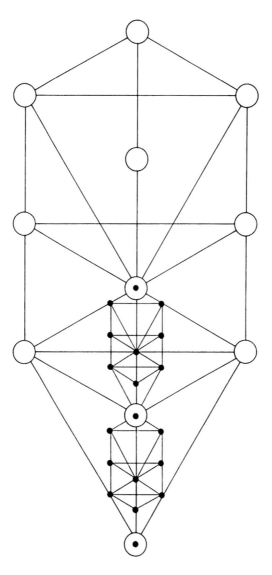

Figure 7   The Triple Tree of Life

or Middle Pillar. This rotation takes the form of a triple spiral, shown by the Three Worlds and the Three Wheels. We may thus allocate trumps upon Lunar, Solar and Stellar levels of the Tree of Life. (See Figure 8.)

The spiritual entity or Higher Self emits a cycle of images upon each of the three levels or spirals, within each of the Three Worlds. Modern psychology has 'discovered' the fact long taught in esoteric traditions, namely that consciousness consists of many images endlessly relating to one another around a central core. This materialist concept of personality, ego and aspects of consciousness corresponds partly to the Lunar World, but omits certain important connectives taught in esoteric tradition, such as the Elements, non-human beings, and psycho-biological energies.

The second spiral, however, is that of an awakened spiritual consciousness in which many processes of cognition and imagination are experienced which are not commonly found in the Lunar World or everyday human life. It is at this level that archetypes are related harmoniously to one another, and the sun, centre of the solar system, is a natural symbol for such a process.

We may meditate upon the Tree of Life and find that eight paths connect to the 6th or Solar Sphere, three of which cross the Abyss into the Stellar World. These Paths represent the archetypes or images that are typical to the consciousness of the Solar World, just as the four connecting to the 9th Sphere represent archetypes of consciousness in the Lunar World. The central locii (the 9th and 6th Spheres) are further defined by threshold or encompassing Paths: the Lunar pattern is that of an inverted triangle, while the Solar pattern is square, and the Stellar polygonal (see Figure 9). This superficially simplistic use of shapes is of major importance in a number of meditations upon form, the Three Worlds, orders of Being, and related concepts.

Who Mediates?

Our short summary of concepts of the Higher Self and Universal Mind in magical arts poses a number of questions. Modern practitioners generally find the subject obscure, and there is a dearth of information and elucidation in published source books. But beyond this merely intellectual level of appraisal and discussion, in which operational patterns are debated and defined, there is a characteristic or exemplary situation, in which we may meet with people who typify some of those same problems and questions. It is a regrettable fact that the fringes of magical arts, such as popular 'occultism' abound with eccentric, imbalanced, weak, egomaniacal men and women; within this crowd we may occasionally encounter examples of domination by telesmatic images or archetypes. It should be stated, however, that this is a fairly rare occurrence, and should not be confused with simple emotional identification or wishful thinking on the part of those who generate an enervating fantasy life as a substitute for their inadequacy or despair. One of the most interesting examples of this type of problem appears in connection with the figure of Merlin. As an author I have researched, written and published worldwide more than any other writer on the figure of Merlin in literature, legend, early texts and bardic or esoteric tradition; yet I do not claim, under any circumstances, to *be* Merlin. I frequently receive letters from people who claim that they are Merlin, or that Merlin has a close or exclusive contact with them, or that they are part of an organisation led or advised by Merlin. Clearly they cannot all be Merlin or all have genuine contact with the real Merlin (who remains an enigma). But the powerful Merlin archetype or image, which takes several related forms, has captured their imagination to various degrees. Those who think that they really are Merlin merely reveal their own weakness or imbalance; those who claim to have contact with Merlin are a small part of a growing revitalisation of the Western Mysteries, within which Merlin is a major figure upon imaginative or inner levels. The context of any such contact can only be judged, of course, upon its own merit rather than upon claims by any individual or group.

Domination by an archetype is known to a limited extent in mental therapy, but domination by a magical form or telesmatic image is of a different order to that of the general images found within the individual or even the collective psyche. In past cultures such domination posed less of a difficulty than it might do today; people attuned to or partially compelled by powerful inner images could become members of a Mystery, a religious

Figure 8   Tarot Trumps upon the Axis Mundi

(Following the cosmology and magical psychology of the Vita Merlini and related systems from tradition. The numbers shown are merely for reference and are not necessarily part of a symbolic system.)

1 *The Moon*   4 *Wheel of Fortune (Boundary of Lunar World)*
2 *The Sun*   5 *Wheel of Justice (Boundary of Solar World)*
3 *The Star*   6 *Wheel of Judgement (Boundary of Stellar World)*

The Ascending or Catabolic Trumps

7 *The Fool*   11 *The Tower*
8 *The Magician*   12 *Death*
9 *The Chariot*   13 *The Hanged Man*
10 *The Guardian (The Devil)*   14 *The Hermit*

The Descending or Anabolic Trumps

15 *The Innocent (Hierophant)*   19 *The Empress*
16 *Temperance*   20 *The Lovers*
17 *The Emperor*   21 *The Priestess*
18 *Strength*   22 *The Universe*

Wheel One: The Lunar World, centred upon the Moon

⊙ *Energy / spirit / transpersonal consciousness*
☽ *Psyche / sexual energies / subconscious and collective or ancestral consciousness*
♀ *Emotions*
☿ *Intellect*
⊕ *Body and outer events*

Wheel Two: The Solar World, centred upon the Sun

⁘ *The Abyss (crossed by trumps of Star, Hanged Man, Temperance)*
⊙ *Transpersonal consciousness*
☽ *Psyche, subconscious (supporting emotions/intellect)*
♂ *Catabolic energies and consciousness*
♃ *Anabolic energies and consciousness*

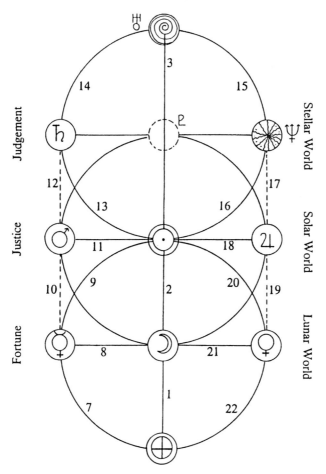

Wheel Three: The Stellar World, centred upon the Unknown Void

◉ *Primum Mobile / seed and first utterance of Being*
⊙ *The Abyss or Void*
⊙ *Transpersonal consciousness (reflects or utters lower consciousness)*
♄ *Universal Understanding*
Ψ *Universal Wisdom*

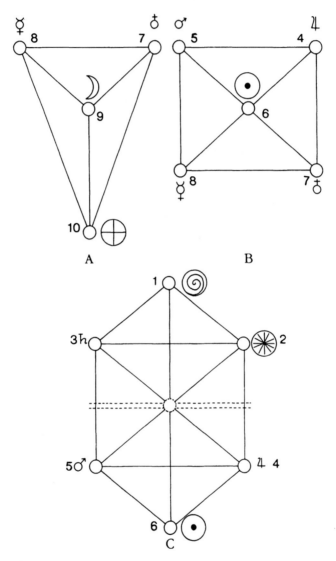

Figure 9   The Three Worlds as Glyphs upon the Tree of Life

A: Lunar   B: Solar   C: Stellar

order, or a magical school of discipline. Within the temple training or similar structure, an individual dominated by an archetype may play an important role as part of a group of specialists.

This method of working is not well suited to modern culture, though we often find traces of it arising in magical groups, particularly when influences from previous lifetimes are brought into consciousness through meditation and ritual work. In time the archetype concerned can be rebalanced through group and individual effort: we can see traces of this in chthonic cults today, where a god or goddess 'inhabits' a person, often a child, for a period of time then departs to another incarnation or host. While this is an important subject in the study of primal religions, it does not apply today in practical magic, other than through certain rare innerworld organisations which still employ such methods.

We should distinguish, of course, between self-acclaimed Celtic bards and Druids, Egyptian Priestesses (inevitably *high* Priestesses), reincarnations of great masters or adepts, and the rare and recognisable phenomenon of true archetype domination. The first group range from amusing fantasies to serious long-term mental imbalance founded in fear and insecurity. The second group has a deeper problem, often enduring for long periods of time, even from one life to another; they may make important contributions to art, literature, science and human culture in general, often at the expense of the personality or 'lower self'.

Without being specific we could suggest that some of the obvious imbalances and problems of the much-publicised occultists of the nineteenth and twentieth centuries were due to archetype domination: hence the quixotic combination of valuable original work with frivolous or even dangerous rubbish.

Such domination seldom arises from properly conducted magical work; it may occur as a result of strong emotional identification combined with magical power such as an actual ritual or at a geomantic locus connected to ancient magico-religious practices. It may also occur as a result of incomplete or improper and unrealised innerworld contact. In other words, the archetype or telesm concerned is incorporated within the *personality*, giving a higher force flowing dangerously through a lower form.

This returns us to our root concept of mediation, for true mediation might be said to be conducted only by the Higher Self, in harmony with the outer personality. Without this spiritual mediation, the consciousness of the Solar World or Harmony, archetype domination may occur. It is only fair to say that what usually occurs, in a case of the personality attempting to inflate itself with a powerful telesmatic image or archetype, is simple failure. This is why magical ceremonies spend so much time upon moving through the worlds of consciousness, for this movement or harmonic transformation attunes the entire being, and enables the energies and telesmatic forms to act harmoniously together. While this may sound rather simple and wonderful in theory, it takes a great deal of hard effort, training and many stern – often devastating – insights and transformations before it can be achieved.

PART TWO

5

EXPERIENCE OF THE UNDERWORLD

Introduction

One of the most neglected yet most important primal magical traditions is that of the UnderWorld.[4] One of the great weaknesses of Western esoteric tradition, partly derived from the long period of influence of orthodox political religion, is that all metaphysical or spiritual realms (known frequently in modern literature as *innerworlds*) are supposed to be 'higher'. In extreme cases we have the very dangerous and debilitating concepts of paradises and heavens that are totally removed from the regular human world and from most other worlds or conceptual realms; such paradises are reserved (of course) for a dogmatic elect.

The UnderWorld tradition stands the entire matter on its head, and offers a paradox that activates many of the deepest levels of folklore, legend and myth. It states, simply, that all power comes from below: that the *deepest* worlds or planes are also the *highest*. A number of illustrations exist which demonstrate this concept, and the standard Tree of Life found in Westernised Kabbalah includes concepts and tuition to this effect, drawn from genuine Jewish mysticism but frequently misunderstood by revival occultists. Our Figure 5 is one way of illustrating the relationship between Worlds that is a major feature of the UnderWorld initiation. Although the familiar modern Tree of Life is incorporated into the illustration, this type of UnderWorld cosmology and magical psychology predates the introduction of Kabbalah into Western Europe.

The concept derives historically from the distant past, but was retained at the heart of folk tradition and Celtic legend well into the nineteenth and twentieth centuries. It has many parallels worldwide which need not be cited here, as this is not a text on anthropology. In the present context we are concerned with the effectiveness of the UnderWorld tradition in magical arts: how it works, what we might do with it in the present day, and how it might be developed for the future. It need hardly be stated that the UnderWorld is not the realm of hell, damnation evil spirits or any similar propagandist negative concept. Certain elements of the popular fictional 'hell', however, are derived from corruptions of older traditions of an energetic but metaphysical realm that could be entered from within the earth, underground, or more subtly through an analogous descent within the consciousness.

In this last context, modern materialist restatements of the unconscious (particularly in the sense defined by C. G. Jung) approach the magical concept, but the UnderWorld begins where the unconscious of modern psychology seems to end, and incorporates many dimensions and entities which are simply not accepted in materialist world-views of any sort. Thus the modern student may gain some preliminary understanding of the UnderWorld through Jung's exploratory definitions in terms of psychology, but magical experience moves far beyond this level.

Psychological theories suffer from the almost irresolvable problem that defining or labelling matters of consciousness does not in any way give true insight; even the therapist's insight gained through experience and intuition may not be passed on by intellectual labelling. Labelling cannot go any way towards replacing actual experience. This problem becomes highly amplified in magical arts, where symbolic alphabets and cycles of myth and legend form a complex technical vocabulary that is most sufficient in its own right, but immediately emasculated by a so-called rational or even psychological 'explanation'. A magical experience, a mode of consciousness, the results of a visualisation, can often be adequately labelled in psychological terms, but we frequently find that only one level of the experience is accommodated by such labelling. No amount of psychological explanation or experiment can compare to the actual experience of transforming consciousness through magical arts.

Of all the practical and powerful traditions existing within magical arts, the UnderWorld is the oldest and most ubiquitous. It occurs within the Grail texts and Gnostic Christianity just as frequently as it occurs in Celtic legend deriving from pagan religion. We find it represented physically in a number of ancient sites and in the temples of the pre-Christian period; we also find it enduring in the concept of the crypt beneath the great churches of Christianity, where perpetual masses were celebrated and the blessed dead were kept. This aspect of the Christian religion is directly derived from the eternal flame, ancestors and underground chambers of pagan religions. The popular rationalisation (based in part upon history) that Christians used to worship secretly in the catacombs of Rome merely reflects a potent and ancient tradition: all true power comes from below. Christ descended into the UnderWorld to liberate the souls of those entrapped there, we are taught, yet many other pagan kings and heroes made similar journeys for similar purposes, so the theme is by no means uniquely Christian. For a cult or religion to have validity, to have regenerative power, it must have its roots in the UnderWorld, no matter in what direction it chooses to grow thereafter.

In a modern context the UnderWorld is particularly important as a corrective to the vapid 'Aquarian' or 'New Age' pseudo-consciousness, in which ease, cosmic-ness, and bland washes of undirected imaginative whimsy totally obviate any inner development, leaving us lost in a welter of superficiality and commercialism. The type of power that arises in UnderWorld visualisations, meditations and rituals totally banishes any cosy illusions regarding spirituality but offers lasting insight and transformation.

The UnderWorld tradition also has a major role to play in revival paganism, for it was the deep source of all pagan philosophy and religion, yet is hardly included in modern attempts to reinstate paganism as a valid alternative to materialism, atheism and moribund orthodox religion. As the Under-World initiation or experience is cathartic and transformative, it provides both concepts and energy for serious development of pagan lore and practice.

Upon the intellectual and scientific levels of modern occultism, the UnderWorld provides a limitless amount of research material. The deeper one goes into the UnderWorld, the further back in time the consciousness seems to penetrate. Material from very early cultures, civilisations and schools of magical art can become available to the questing magician or group by entering the UnderWorld. Furthermore such material does not necessarily appear in the much-popularised manner of 'communications' (so many of which are absurdly trivial and time-wasting) but arises directly within the consciousness as if from personal or ancestral memory. Here is where the Under-World tradition has certain concepts in common with those proposed by C. G. Jung when he described the unconscious as a collective entity enduring through time. But we must not assume that this psychological theory is the sole potential and definition of the UnderWorld for it relates only to the unconscious that is not activated or 'contacted'.

Magical arts enable various levels or worlds of consciousness to interact; hence the UnderWorld experience puts the deepest levels of human consciousness into contact with other entities, known in modern occultism as *innerworld beings*. The innerworld beings in esoteric tradition, particularly that of the UnderWorld, are radically different from the popularised concept of 'spirit guides'; they include ancestral personae or memories, the enduring telesmatic forms of certain gods and goddesses, and specific individuals and groups or orders who inhabit dimensions only accessible through altered states of consciousness. These entities make the general spirit guide or hidden master pale into insignificance. They should, therefore, be approached with some respect and caution.

But we should not succumb to the misleading trend of determining all magical arts in terms of 'communication' and 'entities'; although such matters play a vital and major role in magical work, they are only one part of the overall picture. The UnderWorld tradition, like all magical or spiritual traditions is ultimately one of *power that transforms*. The type of power that is employed in UnderWorld workings is intimately linked both to planetary forces, and to localised power sources on ancient or geomantic sites. This has its human parallel in energies that are aroused by a specific movement of awareness *downwards* through imaginative or magical arts: when the geophysical and human energies are merged, the power is transformed and reappears highly amplified to enliven and awaken or even radically transform those higher centres that are so frequently written of in esoteric instruction, but so little understood or experienced. Having briefly discussed the background and potential of the UnderWorld tradition, let us proceed to our visualisation.

The UnderWorld Visualisation

First we build before us the vision of a door set in an aged stone wall. The wall is overgrown with ivy and moss, and the stones are almost hidden by wild growth. Behind a hanging strand of dark-green ivy, we see a small low door set in an archway. The keystone of the arch is inscribed with a symbol [*See Figure 10*] which we meditate upon briefly . . .

Now we consider the door itself: it is of dark wood, almost black, hard, enduring oak. Upon the door is carved a small image of a bear standing upright, with one paw resting against the trunk of a tree. The tree spreads its branches over the head of the bear, which seems to be turning its head towards us. This is one of the doorways to the UnderWorld, and the Bear is the first guardian upon the way. Before entering the door, we must meditate upon the meaning and power of the Bear . . .

As we meditate, the door slowly opens to reveal a low passageway with stone-lined walls. A small lamp hangs from the corbelled roof, and by the light of this lamp we see a flight of well-made steps sloping gently down. A steady, warm glow radiates from the walls of the stone corridor and the roof just touches our heads as we enter. As we begin to descend we see ahead of us another lamp; we realise that these lamps are fixed at regular intervals along the roof and that it is their light that reflects from the surrounding walls.

Behind us we hear the sound of a door closing, and for a moment it seems as if we also hear a large creature moving outside the door, as if something has come to stand guard and protect our backs. We descend the steps, and the air seems to be growing warmer. The descent is long and we find a steady rhythm to our downward motion, each step being of equal height and width. This even pace carries us onwards until we feel that we are deep underground.

Suddenly our surroundings change: we pass through a hanging curtain of tiny shells, feathers and bones. The well-jointed stonework and the evenly spaced steps cease; above our heads the lamps become less frequent, and we see

Figure 10   The Bear Door

that they have changed into small, crude clay bowls, smoke-blackened, each emitting a gentle golden light from a single wick. The steps are now rough and have shallow depressions in the middle, as if worn by many feet; there is a gradual spiralling of the passageway to the right, and the shaped stones of the walls are replaced by natural rock. The passageway narrows, and we find a stout rope fastened to either wall by heavy bronze spikes. The end of each spike is shaped into the head of a dragon holding the rope in its jaws. As the steps grow steeper, we use this rope to help our descent: in the dim light we see that it is plaited from three smaller ropes, coloured red, white and black.

The rock walls are tinted an iron-red, and seem to be both damp and warm. Ahead we can hear the sound of running water, which grows louder as we spiral round and down. The roof becomes very low and we have to stoop; just as it seems that the passageway is about to close entirely, we squeeze through a narrow gap, and find ourselves in a high-domed circular chamber. At last we can stand freely after the long descent, and we find ourselves upon a smooth, perfectly flat stone floor, cut directly from the natural rock.

All around we hear the sound of flowing water, and the air is hot and moist, with traces of steam, but no water can be seen. The chamber is lit by a large silver lamp hanging from the centre of the roof upon a chain. The lamp is shaped as two intertwined serpents, each with a wick issuing like a tongue from its mouth, joining together to burn as one single flame.

By the light of this lamp, we see that figures are carved out of the rock, reaching from the floor to the roof of the chamber: there are seven figures around the chamber walls. We pause and consider each one, and meditate briefly upon their appearance and meaning. They are in the shape of seven women, each carrying a different object, each looking strangely human yet non-human. Their feet seem to merge into the chamber floor, the very tops of their heads look down out of the roof; above each head is carved a tiny star from which crystals reflect the light. As the figures are of different heights and are placed irregularly around the chamber, the stars form a group or constellation around the central chain with its dragon lamp.

As we meditate upon the carved figures, we hear a slight sound, and then the tapping of a stick upon the stone floor. A figure emerges from behind one of the carvings; he is an aged man, walking with the aid of a silver stick. He has long white hair and a clear, pale face; his eyes reveal a long life of experience and compassion.

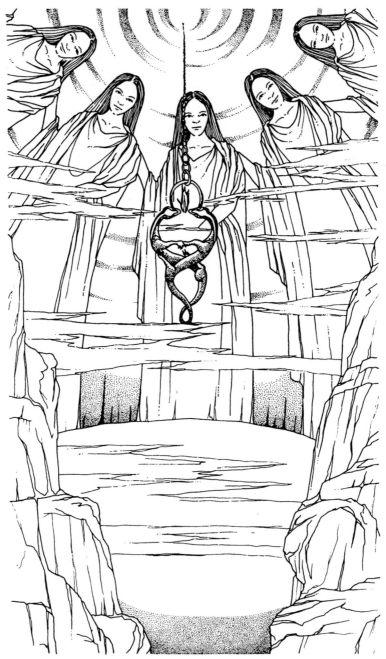

Figure 11   The UnderWorld Chamber

Without pausing to greet us in any way, he indicates that we must immediately follow him, and crosses to the far side of the chamber where he stands against the wall and watches each of us closely as we approach. When it seems that we can go no further, he strikes his silver stick against the foot of one of the carved figures, and a slab of stone tilts upwards behind him to reveal a further passage. As he leads us within, we know that he is the second guardian upon our journey.

The passageway ahead is lit by dim, smoking torches set at irregular intervals into the wall; our guide moves very quickly, and we dare not pause for a moment. The air is now growing hot, and occasionally the entire passageway seems to tremble slightly. Distant deep rumbling sounds are heard, and suddenly our guide pauses at a division of the way.

To our right is a wide, rounded passage, with the rock fused almost into the appearance of glass; from this passage, heat and red light issue and roaring sounds as of a vast creature bellowing in the depths. To our left is a steeply descending passageway of total darkness, and the guide indicates that this is our proper route. He stands to one side and with his silver stick points, first upwards to a sign carved over the doorway, then downwards into the dark.

We approach the entrance, and see that there are many steps glowing very faintly in the shadow, giving just sufficient light for us to feel our way carefully downwards. One by one we enter the passageway, and as we do so the aged man reaches into a plain brown bag hanging at his belt, and quietly gives each of us a small object. There is not enough light to see what this mysterious gift might be, so we keep it safe for the future.

Once the opening of the passageway has been passed, our eyes begin to adjust to the dim, glowing light from the steps, and when we can see enough to proceed, we begin our next level of descent. Behind us, now far above, we hear a solid thud as the stone door from the circular chamber swings closed; we know that our guide has returned to his watch.

At first the steps spiral around tightly to the right, and we turn with almost every step. Occasionally the spiralling stairs still tremble from some deep vibration, and we hear a booming sound that seems almost to contain deep voices chanting or roaring. Down and round the steps turn, round and ever downwards. They become shorter and steeper, merging into one another, until the way ahead turns into a smooth, rapidly descending slope. There are small hand-holds cut into the rock walls on either side: we may choose to slide or crawl.

As we move downwards, the distant roaring fades away and the air cools gradually, until it is fresh and invigorating. Without warning we come upon a long, cyclopean block of roughly hewn stone, making a vast lintel across a low, pitch-dark hole. As we crawl through, we find three huge steps, so steep that we have to climb carefully down each one, feeling our way in the dark, for they are deeper than the height of a man or woman. As we climb down the third and last step, we know that these are all that remain of a temple raised up in the most distant unknown past, and that we have reached the very lowermost point of our long descent into the UnderWorld.

Now we can smell the sea, and hear the lapping of tiny waves upon rock. We see faint light from the distant cavern mouth, and a long stone landing-place cut out of the side wall through which we have climbed. Moored to a stone post, is a small black boat without mast or sails.

Behind us we hear a grinding, shuddering sound as the massive rock lintel slowly lowers itself to seal the passageway. There is no other way but forward, and we must climb into the boat if we are to pass into the UnderWorld sea. We carefully go on board, each taking a seat until the vessel is balanced; then we pause to contemplate the unseen ocean that lies ahead in the light. [*Here, music may be played.*]

The vessel moves and we are carried forward towards the cavern mouth, slowly at first but with increasing speed. The water slaps against the prow, then builds into a rushing wave that foams past, flashing with phosphorescent colours in the dimness of the cavern. The arch of light ahead grows closer, larger, brighter, until we break out suddenly into a wide, sunlit sea.

The waters are green and blue, with many strange fishes sporting and leaping from their depths; great flocks of birds wheel and cry above us, and in the distance we see a chain of tiny islands. Looking up at the flying birds, and the bright sunlit sky, we see to our amazement a full panoply of stars. All the constellations shine strongly, accompanied by a full sun and full moon, and each planet glowing like a jewel with a different colour. This is the sky of the sun at midnight, where light and dark, night and day, are perfected in one another . . .

As we watch the stars swirl and move far above us, we realise that the vessel has ground to a halt, her bows resting lightly on a pebbled beach. Before us a steep island rises, set about with many tall standing-stones. We climb from the boat, which slides back into the waves, and slowly heads out to sea. The island is silent, with only the sound of the waves swirling gently about its beach. There is a faint path that leads between two tall standing-stones, and we see a familiar constellation positioned exactly over the gap between the stones; this is the path that we must follow.

As we approach the stones, a figure in a long cloak and deep hood appears from behind the left-hand stone. Her cloak is of deep black, lined with red, and her face is stern, partly hidden in the shadow of her hood. She stands before us and holds out a plain wooden bowl, chipped and cracked with age. We know that she is asking each of us for the unseen gifts given by the old man in the distant circular chamber, and we take out these objects for the first time, and see them by the light of the midnight sun and stars. Each one of us has a small disc of coloured stone, and on it is an image representing that which we are most attached to in our lives; this image may be surprising, for it is sometimes not what would be expected.

To pass through the gateway of the upright standing-stones, we must give our tokens to She Who Waits. One by one the brightly coloured engraved gemstones fall into the dull wooden bowl, and as the last stone is dropped in, we see a sudden transformation. The dirty, cracked begging bowl seems to flow and twist in the hands of the hooded figure: she opens her arms and it hangs for a moment in the air, suddenly radiating light, set about its rim with jewels, engraved with gold and silver and crystal. The vessel emits a complex musical tone, made of many harmonics weaving together; we see that the patterns are those of the constellations, and the jewels on the rim are the sun, moon and planets. For a moment it seems to grow and dissolve simultaneously, then with a last chime, both the bowl and its bearer vanish. We are left to pass freely through the gate, and we find a long, meandering path leading to the centre of the island.

The path weaves between many marker stones of different sizes and colours: some are tall menhirs of green granite, others are crude unshapen boulders, while other tiny crystalline rocks have delicate symbols carved upon them. The rambling convoluted way leads between marker stones from different ages and cultures, in a web that we cannot fully understand, sometimes doubling back upon itself, yet always leading towards the centre of the island. We follow the path carefully until we reach a single huge upright stone, in the very centre of the island. It points directly to a small cluster of stars, and here at last we rest on the heather, grasses, and tiny white and yellow flowers that grow in that place. Lying back, looking up at the cluster of stars, we meditate upon this central sacred stone, our position of rest. [*A short period of silence is allowed here.*]

As the stars wheel overhead, they seem to merge slowly into one another, until their revolving patterns blur and fuse together into a sequence of silver, blue and grey. This flowing colour surrounds us and gradually solidifies into a circular chamber above our heads, in which seven carved figures lean over, seeming to look curiously down upon us.

We find that we are lying in a circle upon the floor of the rock chamber that we left so long ago. At first we see only the carved figures with their calm, strange faces, then we realise that there is someone standing in the centre of the circle, behind our heads just out of immediate sight. We rise to our feet, and turn to look upon a youth, who seems at first male, then female. We find it difficult to look fully at this youth, for he or she shimmers and changes face and colour. As the young one smiles we feel a surge of power and take joy in something nameless, yet utterly known to us all. There is the sound of a chiming bell [*here a small gong or bell may be struck*] and the youth reaches up towards the dragon lamp: as he stretches his hands to the lamp, we hear a great roaring and hissing from the tunnels below and the sound of a huge creature stirring. The chamber shakes and the seven carved figures seem to move their heads to look towards the youth and the dragon lamp.

For a moment we see both a male and female figure unified within the youth, until the beauty becomes unbearable, and we cover our eyes with our hands. Instantly the roaring ceases, and we look again to find ourselves in an empty chamber. The youth has vanished, but the dragon lamp has turned from silver to gold, and the double flaming wicks have become a single blazing crystal. We pause to meditate upon this source of light from the mineral world.

Now the aged keeper of the chamber emerges from behind one of the stone figures. He firmly taps each of us upon the back with his gold and crystal rod, and we know that it is time to return to the outer world. We turn towards the ascending steps, and make our long climb back to the tiny wooden door far above. It opens easily, and as we emerge we find that we are in a great garden, which seems to be a long-familiar place.

The garden is a curious fusion of cultivation and wild forest:

there are countless varieties of trees, and flowering plants, and all kinds of fruit and herbs and flowers. Many creatures pass to and fro through this forest garden, many birds fly overhead and perch within the branches: none show any fear of us. In the far distance, down a long avenue of oak trees lit golden and red by the setting sun, we see a shambling bear walking beside a tall man. The man wears a many-coloured cloak of leaves and is crowned with a head-dress of spreading antlers; he seems to lean towards the bear for a moment, as if they are talking to one another. We long to follow them, but they are already far away, and by nightfall we must return to the human world.

Beneath the nearest trees a circle of carved chairs is set; the carvings show tiny pictures of dragons, tunnels, a dark boat and a wave-filled sea with many stars overhead. These images surround the figure of a dancing youth, or perhaps it is a maiden, with outstretched arms, carved into the centre of each chair-back. We examine the chairs carefully, and we each find one that is fitting, for they vary in size and shape, and each one has a different symbol somewhere upon it that we know and recognise as our own. The sun sets, and gradually the birds fall quiet, and peace descends upon the great garden forest. [*A pause is made here.*] We finally open our eyes and return to our point of starting; faintly in the distance we hear the closing of a door, and we return to the outer world. [*Music may be played here if required.*]

6

EXPERIENCE OF THE WEAVER

Introduction

Serious undertakings in magic cannot be approached or achieved without experience of two closely related concepts: the UnderWorld and the Goddess. Although we have used the word *concepts* the UnderWorld and the Goddess are fundamental and universal powers. They are presentations or modulations of the unknowable One Being, the ultimate reality and truth beyond expression. There are many ways of expressing the UnderWorld and the Goddess, but no amount of discussion replaces actual experience.

Both of these primal concepts and powers have been ignored and suppressed with terrible, possibly irreparable, effect upon both humanity and the planet Earth. Understanding the Goddess leads to sexual balance and maturity upon all levels of consciousness, including those that transcend gender. Understanding of the UnderWorld brings a conscious relationship between humankind and the land, environment and planet. As the Goddess always dwells within the UnderWorld, we should not separate the two in our imagination.

The language of magic may seem archaic and superficially clumsy in terms of materialistic logic, but linear thought processes are insufficient for expression of many magical concepts which require analogous or poetic form as words; the Goddess and the UnderWorld represent energies and consciousness essential to our individual, collective and manifest well-being. Moreover these two concepts and powers have the potential to rebalance our humanity and our collective world, both of which are in immediate undeniable danger of extinction. In very basic terms we may see the nuclear problem, both civil and military, as a result of ignorance and abuse of UnderWorld powers; we may see the grotesque extremes of materialism and male stereotypical (rather than archetypical) dominance as a result of suppression of Goddess powers. These are both very obvious and in many ways superficial examples and reductions of a highly complex and vitally important problem of imbalance in our world at large.

Practical magic, as opposed to theoretical or literary occultism, must work with the Goddess power. This was realised by the revival occultists of the nineteenth and early twentieth centuries, just as it had been understood by the adepts of the Rosicrucian movement, the alchemists, and the Renaissance magicians and metaphysicians. But only one or two generations ago, Goddess workings were unusual in occult orders, though not unknown. Magical arts were still dominated by savage phantoms of male egocentric 'authority' and dogmatic 'hierarchy', phantoms which have by no means been exorcised at the present time. Such male-dominated groups tended or tend to work with the Goddess only in her Venus or sexual loving aspect, because this is close to the pernicious stereotype of pseudo-femininity to which they were conditioned from childhood. As we emerge from a period of monosexual religion and culture, such stereotypical imagery is beginning to be replaced by something new, yet essentially ancient and primal and enduring.

Social conditions change slowly, and often express transformations which were once limited to exploration by magical groups of earlier generations. Thus the restoration of sexual equality is now a widespread social and political issue in the Western world whereas at the turn of the century equality was often a highly daring experiment in which men and women worked magic together (as opposed to the exclusively male Masonic Orders from which the occult groups often derived). The pioneering feminist activist Annie Besant, for example, was one of a number of people who drew their social and political inspiration from esoteric sources. More significant than the mere fact that men and women were working equally at magical arts, though this was a major step forward in itself, were the Goddess-orientated rituals and visualisations that began to appear, often drawing on material from earlier cultures and religions.

Further discussion of the explosion of Goddess worship and various aspects of active feminism in revival paganism are not relevant in a book of this sort; nevertheless one of the most astonishing of the many wonders appearing in the twentieth century is the irresistible return of the Goddess, regardless of her forms of expression. Only a generation ago students heard whispered secrets concerning 'sex magic' in which something unspeakably mysterious occurred between men and women (and it was not sexual intercourse!). The entire science of polarity magic has now opened out and is become increasingly defined and intelligible. Such developments could not occur, in the magical or poetical sense, without the active power of the Goddess restoring our awareness to a balanced condition.

In Western esoteric tradition, as in the East, there are a wide range of what are nowadays called *feminine archetypes*. They are preserved in legend, myth, folklore and in magical, alchemical, and mystical allegory, including the heretical Grail legends. Such archetypes have been banished, often unsuccessfully, from political orthodox religion, though they frequently resurface in the form of female saints who replace pagan goddesses, or as folklore and popular superstition, and revivals of the cult of the Virgin Mary.

More important than any of the sources listed is the inner tradition of making contact with telesmatic images of goddesses, through mediation, visualisation and ritual. It is quite facile and inaccurate to suggest that the West has no goddesses and that such images can play no part in mystical or magical work, but a clear definition and firm contact with such images is often difficult to establish, due to centuries of orthodox suppression and conditioning. Once the contacts have been made, however, the Goddess is an undeniable force, and experienced as a powerful presence in magical rituals.

In advanced magical arts there are two aspects of the Goddess that are especially relevant and potent. We might call them She Who Dwells Below, the Goddess of the UnderWorld, the Dark Mother, and She Who Dwells Above, the universal Goddess of the Stars. They are extremes of one unity, and are found in practical terms to be very close to one another when we visualise or meditate upon them; but they are not interchangeable in a facile manner through human arbitration.

The Western tradition has a *Shortened Way* to enlightenment, which has much in common with similar methods found in Tibetan Buddhism or Zen, though there is no suggestion here that they are identical, or that we should turn to Eastern variants when we already have well-defined and powerful initiatory techniques of our own. The similarities are due to shared properties of human consciousness; the differences are due to ancestors, environment and psychic patterns, all of which are transcended only by working with and moving through a native tradition to its very end.

The Shortened Way simply consists of going into the UnderWorld and encountering the Goddess. For many people this is a terrifying experience to be avoided at all costs: such people should not be involved in magical arts, or if they do become so involved, they soon abandon the effort, or become side-tracked into the various self-perpetuating dead-ends of 'Aquarian' occultism or New Age cosiness and mutual congratulation. These may seem like hard words, but no growing experience, no transformation, is ever easy. By descending into the UnderWorld we are paradoxically reaching towards comprehension and experience not only of the Dark Goddess, the Power of Taking and Giving, but also of Her universal stellar aspect. First the catabolic destroying force that we fear, which is the Dark Goddess, then her universal aspect beyond all concepts of selfhood or false limitation. In this second phase we comprehend the Goddess as a conscious power permeating all time, space and energy.

We find the imagery for this Goddess in various forms in myth and legend, and such imagery is particularly active upon inner levels of visualisation and contact. In our present context we can exclude intermediary forms such as culture goddesses, love goddesses, sister goddesses, war goddesses and specific localised female deities: these are strung like beads upon a cord that reaches from the UnderWorld to the Stars. During the UnderWorld initiation, we realise that the linear concept of this cord is an illusion, and that both ends are one, giving us the image of a circle or sphere. This sphere contains the universe in one dimension, and the planet or UnderWorld in another: the Goddess weaves all dimensions and energies together.

In human terms, this power is found both beneath and
within, a practical matter of the direction of energy and
consciousness through ritual and imaginative constructs such as
goddess-forms and guided visualisations. To our ancestors
there was an eminently simple method: they went underground
into chambers, caves and catacombs, and sought enlightenment. This physical movement is analogous to a visionary
transformative experience in which we enter a realm beneath
the earth, yet find that it is full of stars. In both Celtic and Greek
mythology, we find the goddess known as the Weaver, and She
appears in several important magical or mystical visions.[2] The
visualisation which follows employs many aspects of the
Goddess tradition, showing the Weaver in one of her most
potent primal aspects.

The Weaver Visualisation

We begin by meditating upon a single candle flame. [*A candle
or slow-burning nightlight is lit here.*] We look upon this light,
firstly with open eyes, and know that it represents the
spiritual light that burns within us. This light is everywhere,
with its origin and centre within all and any chosen time,
space or being. As we meditate upon the light, we close our
eyes, and remain in formless contemplation for a few
moments. [*A short, silent pause here.*]

Now we see before us a vision of three rings or circles,
interlaced to form a sphere. One ring is vertical, one
horizontal, one fully open towards us. As we look upon these
rings they rotate slowly, each taking the place of the other.
They seem to flow and merge into one another, and at the
same time turn with their own motion. As we look upon this
mystery, the rings expand and pass beyond our view, moving
through and over us until we are within them, yet grown so
vast that they are unseen.

We find ourselves standing upon a warm, sunny square or
courtyard. The air is scented with summer perfumes from
many exotic plants; we see a huge stone wall of tightly fitting
massive blocks of masonry . . . a flowering tree grows up the
wall, its huge white and red blooms open wide to the hot
sunlight. We have never seen a tree of this type before . . . its
trunk is smooth dark-green with deep-black markings, and the
leaves are wide and shining with a rich deep-blue colour shot

Figure 12   The Weaver

with grey-green tints. A tiny breeze stirs the wide white and
red flowers, and they rustle gently.

   With the sound of the light wind in the leaves and blossoms,
we hear a faint footfall, and turn to see a boy come towards us.
He is no more than a child, dressed in a plain white tunic, as if
he is a pupil or novice. He solemnly beckons to us, and leads
us towards a square doorway in the wall. A plain stone slab
tilts upwards to admit us to a cool, dark building: we pass
within and the heat and scents of summer, the perfume of the
strange tree, immediately vanish. The interior of the building
is cool and silent. We find that we are in a large chamber, lit by
high slits, near to the roof, through which shafts of dim light
pass, filtered through windows or membranes that shade it
pale green and blue. At the far end of this place is a wide
circular well, into which a flight of steps descends. Our guide
leads us with a steady, formal pace, towards the stair-well,
and when we reach the first step, he chimes upon a small
bronze bell suspended from a single carved stone shaped like
the fine stem of a plant with an opening blossom.

   A clear, deep note sounds through the chamber, and the
boy sits cross-legged beneath the stone flower and vibrating
bell. We pause, and see that someone is already ascending the
steps to meet us . . . he is an old man in a long dark-red robe
with a curious symbol embroidered upon it. He reaches the
top of the stairs, and looks carefully at each of us in turn. He
holds a large ball of multicoloured twine in his hand, and
suddenly throws it so that it rolls down the steps and out of
sight, unwinding as it falls. We hear the soft sound of the ball
passing from step to step, rapidly. The old man holds the end
of the twine, which he passes to one of us when the sound of
the ball fades and can be heard no more. He then sits
cross-legged opposite the boy, on the other side of the
stairwell. We know that we must descend between them,
following the line of the ball of twine.

   As we descend the steps, we realise that we are climbing
down into a vast cavern, so great that we cannot measure its
size. It is lit by a dim radiance reflected from the walls, though
we cannot see the source of the light. Our stair, which seemed
so huge when we entered upon it, clings to the edge of one
wall, and descends like a tiny ledge into the depths. The
thread runs straight ahead of us, and we follow it, hand over
hand, loosely, letting it lie upon the stairs behind reaching up
into the chamber far above.

   When we finally arrive at the foot of the long flight of steps,
we find that we are standing upon a level stone floor, and that

the line of twine suddenly turns, rolling away in a wide curve to our right. We follow it, and feel that we are travelling in a great circle . . . soon the wall and the stairs are left behind. Our footsteps echo back to us very faintly, seeming to come from far away, and suddenly the twine seems like a lifeline; without it we have no idea where we are going, and without it we would not be able to find our way back to the stairs. We follow the twine, and feel that we are walking in a spiral so vast that we have hardly begun to cover one turning. The roof of the cavern is lost to sight above us; looking up we seem to fall into a dizzy pit of shadow. Soft radiance seems to fill the air around us, then recedes as if breathing in and out.

As we walk we slowly become aware of a firm light, as if from a lamp or fire, and a solid shape like a black circle or disc beyond that light. Our thread is leading us to this. The shape is still far away, but our movement over the smooth stone floor is rapid and steady, and the disc seems to come towards us. So huge is the surrounding space that we have no way of judging relative proportions.

As we draw closer to the disc, we see that it is made of glass or polished black stone. It is a perfect circle of reflecting blackness, many times the height of a man, seeming to float without support, balanced upon its edge, which just touches the stone floor. By the side of this vast mirror is a tall silver-coloured stand shaped like an upright serpent, and from its mouth a clear flame burns. We draw closer to the mirror and the lamp, and see that the serpent stand is not of silver, but of crystal. The flame seems to appear from nowhere out of the serpent's mouth; we can see no oil or wick to supply it. In the vast black mirror, we see a reflection of ourselves, softly lit by the crystal lamp. We seem small, almost pitiful in the vast dreaming shadows of the cavern.

Looking upon the circular disc, with its glassy black polished face, we realise that within it we can see a shape, beyond our personal reflections, as if it shows something behind or beyond us. We strive to see this shape, yet it eludes us . . . the closer we look, the further away it seems to fade. We stand back and try to focus upon what is hidden in the depths of the great black mirror. As we do so, we become aware of someone standing near to the mirror edge, on the side opposite the crystal serpent; a figure steps into the light and we see that it is a woman in a long black robe and deep hood, who had been hidden from us in the shadows. She carries a long staff, with a thread spiralling around it, and we feel a sense of terrible power emanating from her. She seems to glide across the floor towards us, and raise her staff high above her head: in an instant she strikes the serpent lamp, and it shatters into many pieces. We are plunged into total darkness, so complete that we seem to be falling.

As we fall we see a circle suddenly illuminated below us, and we realise that we are falling into the black mirror, which has now become light. We fall through into a rocky cave, brightly lit by many tiny lamps burning in niches and crevices all around. We tumble onto the floor, and for a moment see nothing but the stone roof and the tiny lamps. We realise that we are at the feet of a vast, dark figure, and we stand to look upon it. It is a woman, towering above us, carved of black polished stone. She sits with her head tilted slightly downwards, as if looking at us. Her face is huge and calm, showing no human emotion. Her arms are outstretched, and we see that a thick strand of rope falls from one hand towards the floor, while another reaches from her other hand up into the cavern roof, where it vanishes away through the rock. Only then do we realise that she is not looking at us, but at a picture carved into the floor of the cave. The rope that descends sinks through the stone, and merges into an image of a loom, upon which we have fallen. The rope leading upwards passes through another picture of a loom carved into the roof, and we see a mirror image of the floor below, with tiny spirals and shapes in the weaving.

This was the place seen in the dim image just visible in the black mirror before the breaking of the crystal serpent lamp. We pause to meditate upon the figure of the goddess, and upon her Mystery. [*A pause for silent meditation here.*]

As we sit and meditate upon the meaning of the vast goddess image and her double loom, a young woman in a white robe enters the cave, and begins to tend the lamps: each lamp has its wick trimmed until the flame burns brightly. She pays no attention to us, but as she passes round the chamber walls, and tends each lamp, we feel a cleansing clarifying power at work within us. Even as she trims the lamps, the light increases, until the entire chamber is filled with brilliant illumination. The giant black goddess figure is surrounded by a halo of light; the thick strands of twisted rope shimmer in her hands, and rotate with spiralling changes of colour. The loom pattern, inlaid into the floor where we sit, seems to move and change configuration. We look upwards to the chamber roof and see that the loom above changes also, then slowly fades away into a pattern of stars cut deeply into the stone.

We are drawn by these carved patterns of stars, in great spirals and complex shapes; we stand, and find that as we rise the black goddess slowly fades from sight, vanishing into the brilliance of the lamps. As we reach our feet, we hear a gong chime [*gong sound here if possible*] and know that the maiden has finished trimming the lamps. As the echoes of the gong fade away, the roof of the chamber, with its patterns of stars, begins to crack open and divide into two parts. The right- and left-hand halves of the roof slowly pull apart, revealing a night sky filled with shining constellations. At the very centre of this sky is a moving coil of stars, a whirlpool of light turning inwards and outwards in a double spiral.

From the surface above, a simple wooden ladder is slowly lowered down to us; we see an aged man and a child on either side of the ladder, their faces looking down at us briefly. When we begin to climb, they retreat out of our line of sight. One by one we reach the ladder top and climb out to find ourselves on the summit of a high round hill. Lamplight shines out of the hole from which we have climbed, but light from the double spiral of stars increases, moves and grows until we can see nothing else.

Within the centre of the spiral there is a cloudy veil shimmering and pulsing before a partly hidden figure. As the veil thins momentarily, we see a woman in a silver-grey robe, with a deep hood totally covering her face. In her hand she holds a distaff, from which a spiralling thread twists and turns until it becomes the double coil of stars. [*See the trump of Judgement in the Merlin Tarot for this image.*]

The veil grows thin, and without knowing why, we find that we have already bowed our heads and covered our eyes with our hands. We remain in silence and experience the power of the great Goddess as she spins, weaves and unweaves. [*Silent meditation here.*]

Now we feel a change, a movement beneath our feet, as if the hilltop had tilted momentarily. The air grows warmer, and is filled with strange rich scents. We sense sunlight upon our faces and when we lower our hands to look, find that we are back in the sunlit courtyard, standing by the tree with its huge blooms and strangely coloured leaves. Upon the courtyard floor, we see for the first time, a large woven carpet. It is coloured red, white and black, and contains many abstract patterns and connecting lines and shapes. Upon the carpet are some stone balls, seemingly thrown at random. We feel strongly drawn to play this ball-throwing game, but as we turn towards the carpet, the old priest in his red robe appears from behind the tree, and forbids us to approach or touch anything, making a curious sign with his hands. We try to remember this sign, for it is part of the inner temple language. He directs us away from the carpet and its entrancing pattern, and shows us instead a low square door in the wall beside the tree. The door has a thick lintel and capping stone, and even as we look at it, the stone slab from which it is made tilts upwards, revealing a dimly lit familiar room. At first it looks like a shadow room within a dream, but gradually it takes on substance and colour. We pass through the stone door, and sit, each in his or her familiar chair. There is a sound of grinding stone, and as the door closes, our vision of the temple courtyard wall fades away. As we return to the outer world, we each discover that we have been given a token, by one of the people encountered upon our journey. This token appears in our hands, and we study it for a moment, immediately knowing who gave it to us and reflecting upon its meaning. These tokens will enable us to return to the innerworlds through which we have travelled in seeking the Weaver Goddess. But as each token is different, and was given by a different guardian, we cannot know or presume where they will ultimately lead.

But it is now time to redirect our vision, and return to the outer world, bringing with us the light and the knowledge that we have gained within.

7

THE MYSTERY OF THE VAULT

Introduction

This visualisation is based closely upon one of the enduring motifs found in Western magical and mystical tradition. In its simplest form it consists of a vision of a person, usually but not inevitably male, lying in a chamber or vault. We find it as a central image in the Grail legends, in Rosicrucian symbolism, and in the later intellectual developments of nineteenth-century occultism through the profound influence of the Golden Dawn, drawing from various literary, Masonic and visionary sources.

There seems little doubt that the motif is part of a pagan life, death and resurrection mystery; it has classical and Celtic parallels, and is found in primal magical arts worldwide as an initiatory technique. In our context of Western esoteric disciplines, the motif bridges pagan and primal Christian Mysteries: it partakes both of the UnderWorld tradition and techniques of altering consciousness, and of that most significant revelation of Christianity, the Resurrection. The motif of resurrection is found in many pre-Christian and non-Christian religions, so it cannot be claimed as an exclusively or originally Christian theme or revelation. But the Christian context, fused with its pagan origins and expressions, is of considerable importance in Western magical arts, even if the practitioners are not orthodox Christians.

Magicians are well aware that certain images and symbols work powerfully even if their outer religious context is corrupt:

the vision of the chamber of resurrection is one such potent image. It cuts across time and dogma, and attunes the imagination to an eternal theme, rooted deeply into human consciousness. Thus we begin with an essentially pagan visualisation, but it may move in a number of remarkable directions; like the Grail legends which are rooted in this type of imagery, it may never define the wounded figure as Christ; he becomes Christian Rosencreutz in later developments, the model for a new Adam.[14]

It is significant that traditional versions of the motif reveal the chamber and the figure lying within, but do not deal with the resurrection. This curious state may be nothing more than the result of Christian suppression, in which the theme of wounding or suffering was retained in oral tradition, but the subsequent cure and resurrection were lost due to their heretical similarity to orthodox dogma. It is clear, however, that even in the highly developed Grail texts, the resurrection is promised, even implicit, without being tightly attached to State religion.

Our visualisation follows the traditional sequence closely as described in the carol Down in Yon Forest from British folk tradition (see Appendix for typical text). Our primal source, therefore, is not heavily coloured by literary or dogmatic development, but is drawn directly from collective oral tradition and imagination. The fine details, however, are added from related traditional and visionary or inner sources. This method can be very productive indeed when assembling both visualisations and rituals.

It seems likely that this sequence, used extensively in various forms by magical orders for centuries, is known in one way or another to all magical traditions worldwide. The basis of all initiation is that of death to one world and birth into another. Dedicated work with this type of vision and associated ritual practices attunes an individual or group to a specific and enduring innerworld Mystery. We have discussed the concepts of the 'Higher Self' and 'Universal Mind' in Chapter 4; and the motif employed in The Hall in the Forest is closely connected to those transformations that result in contact with a universal consciousness.

The Hall in the Forest

We see before us, with our inner vision, a flowing stream,[15] passing rapidly from right to left. The water is clear and fast-moving, and there are many stones just below the surface. We see that this is a ford or crossing-place, and that the stones were laid to make crossing possible for travellers. Each stone is carved with a letter, sign or sigil worn smooth by the passage of the water: the entire bed of the stream shows a strange alphabet cut into the stones. As we look at these letters, shimmering and wavering in the flow of the waters, a large trout swims upstream rapidly, and we hear a sudden beating of wings.

Looking up, we find that a heron has landed upon the opposite bank. She is coloured grey, and tilts her head to look at us with her wide staring eye. We meditate briefly upon the meaning of the river, the ford, and the watching heron. As we meditate upon the heron, she rises slowly into the air, and begins to climb. Our vision flies with her, and it is as if we see with her eyes as she flies over the land.

Beyond the river bank is a winding road leading to a walled city, in which we see a tall castle with shining towers. But the heron turns aside from this place, and flying on, heads towards a distant dark-green forest. She flies slowly and steadily, beating her long grey wings; seeing through her eyes, flying with her, we see the trees approaching. First there are the scattered outlying small trees and bushes, and we can see small animals running to and fro in the undergrowth; many different kinds of bird fly close to the heron as if to challenge her, but they turn away and leave her free to proceed, for the power of the Great Goddess protects her upon this flight.

Now she flies over the green forest, with tall spreading trees reaching into the sunlight: this is one of the great ancient forests, and we can see only the rolling spread of the treetops, for the branches and foliage are so dense that the ground below is invisible. We can feel a curious heat emanating from the trees as the heron skims their huge crowns, as if the entire domain is a living being radiating vitality. There is a sense of being watched from below, but the heron flies on steadily, heading straight for her unknown destination.

Below us we see a clearing with a herd of deer running swiftly across it, followed by the shadow of the heron made huge in the sunlight. As they move under the tree cover, we catch a short glimpse of a man in a cloak of red leaves, carrying a tall spear. He looks up at us, and we see that he has long, flowing red hair and beard, he wears a garland of ivy leaves and berries, and wide-spreading antlers grow from his head. In an instant he vanishes from sight, stepping under the trees to follow the deer.

The shape of the land changes now, and begins to undulate; low hills covered in trees come into view, and occasionally a hilltop breaks out of the forest. Below we see a bare rocky summit, with a copious spring flowing out to run in streams down into the dense forest below. Many animals come to the spring to drink, and to lick at the red salty earth. We see deer, rabbits, foxes, even a wolf, and then the hilltop is behind us and we fly on.

Now it seems that the heron is looking to right and left, turning and tilting her head, and suddenly we cross a ruined dry-stone wall, that seems to stretch across the entire forest, curving gently as if it forms part of a vast circular enclosure so immense that we cannot see its limits. Many of the stones are tumbled, and the wall is overgrown with moss and ivy, yet it was once a great work, and it is still formidable even in decay.

The trees change now, and we find that they are planted in regular rows: looking down we see that these are short, cultivated trees, and that all are withering or dead. We realise that it is a huge dying orchard, with fruit trees decaying and rotting beneath us as we fly. Some are fallen, others are twisted into strange gnarled shapes. Many are bare of leaves, while others are covered in dry brown foliage, as if a sudden frost had hit them and destroyed all life. The heron picks up speed now, as if she knows that she approaches the end of her long flight.

Deep within the dead orchard, we see a large woooden hall, made of massive timbers carved and tinted with many colours. But the vivid gilding and painting has long since been worn away by rain, sun and wind, and the wood shows through in grey weathered patches. Many of the great roof shingles, cut from broad tree planks, are loose or fallen, and dead leaves swirl over the high peak and the proud eagles carved above each gable window.

Now the heron descends, and she lands before the tall doorway of the hall. We see two immense pillars, each cut from the single trunk of a giant tree, and raised up without planing or carving to frame the entrance. Across these trunks, a third huge tree is laid to form a lintel, complete with thick, gnarled bark and the stumps of great limbs shorn off. This triple gate of trees was raised up before the hall was built, and the elaborate work of the building was assembled upon its enduring frame.

As we look at the giant doorposts, right and left, each seems to be in the form of a figure, as if the natural shape of the trees resembles a formidable man and woman. Yet when we look closely they seem to be trees again. Now we find ourselves standing before the doorway to that hall within the dying orchard, and the sound of beating wings fades into the distance behind us as the heron flies home to her watching place by the ford.

We look upon the doors of the hall; in contrast to the rough-hewn massive pillars on either side and the rugged trunk of the lintel they are deeply and ornately carved, set with many metals and crystals. But all is tarnished and weathered as if abandoned long ago. We see images of many stories set into the panels of the door; some we know well, but others involve places, people and creatures that seem to belong to other worlds, other times. Before we can examine these scenes closely, a great gust of wind hurls leaves and twigs against us, and buffets the doors until they open inwards. In the far distance we hear the faint echo of a horn blowing and the blast of wind throws us against the doors. We hurry into the narrow opening, seeking shelter: as we enter within we hear the thundering sound of riders outside; the wind rises to a high roaring gale, and the horn is sounded again twice. In the sudden silence which follows, we hear the sound of many creatures gradually approaching; we hear hooves, and wings beating, and we hear footsteps and murmuring faint calls and voices. A great host passes as if following the unseen riders.

The hall within is deep in purple shadow, a rich dark light that tints everything it touches. Now all is silent, and we look about us to see long purple drapes hanging from the high roof beams, filtering the sunlight that shines in through the many tiny windows high above. In this sombre light, we can see a raised platform at the far end of the hall, and we pause before walking towards it.

As we grow accustomed to the quiet, after the howling of the wind and the passage of the riders and their followers, we can hear a faint, steady sound of running water. On either side of the great hall, channels are cut in the earthen floor; we see water running bright and clear to our right, while to our left a dark slow-moving stream flows out towards the door. Both streams vanish into deep wells at the foot of the massive door trees, and we hear a very faint sound as if they fall an immense

Figure 13   The Hall in The Forest

distance into the depths below. We meditate upon this falling sound, and hear many distant echoes and intimations from the mysterious place below that receives the streams . . .

Now we move towards the platform that fills the far end of the hall: a single ray of sunlight penetrates the shadows, and shines briefly upon the platform. We see there a large wide bed, hung about with red and purple drapes; the bed is framed by three posts cut from tree branches; the left-hand post is pure white, the right hand post is blood-red, while the horizontal branch that joins them is a pure emerald green. The ray of sunlight slowly fades, as if obscured by a cloud; we ascend the three steps leading to the platform, and look upon the figure lying on the bed. A great sorrow fills us, for he is deeply wounded.

He is both young and old; his face is fair, and his long silver-white hair has grown down over his shoulders. His eyes are closed, and we see no sign of life. He wears a long white robe over silver armour, and an empty scabbard lies by his side. As we approach him, we see that he is breathing very faintly, very slowly, His sides are pierced by a great wound, as if a spear had been thrust through him; we stand before a rent in the robe and armour and flesh that flows with deep-red-black blood. From his other side we see a stream of crystal-clear water flowing down over the edge of the bed; this double wound is the source of the two streams that pass through the hall and fall away into unknown depths beneath the door-trees. We stand in silence, and meditate upon the sleeping knight, his double wound, and the terrible sorrow of that place. [*Music may be played here.*]

As we meditate, we realise that we are not alone in the hall. By the side of the bed, we see a huge hound, white with red-tipped ears. It droops its head, and occasionally licks the bloody wound, as if trying to cure the knight in the only way that it knows. This hound looks directly at us, and we dare not approach more closely, for it guards the wounded knight.

In the shadows, where the water flows over the edge of the bed, we see a young woman sitting with her head bowed. At first we think she may be weeping, but we can see that she holds a corner of the knight's robe, and has a needle and thread in her hands; the thread shines with faint silver light, and we realise that she is sewing. She is dressed in a black robe edged with gold, and by her side a huge broken sword lies upon the stone platform. We dare not look upon her face, hidden in the heavy purple shadows, yet we know that she is very beautiful and terrible.

We pause to meditate upon the meaning of the hound and the maiden, and a deep silence falls upon the hall. [*Silent pause here, terminated by three bell chimes.*] With the chiming of a tiny bell, we hear a wind rising outside, and a clear sunbeam breaks through the gloom from a tiny slit over the distant doorway: it shines the length of the hall onto the head of the bed, where we see a small, twisted thorn tree with dry, dead branches.

The sunbeam shines steadily upon the thorn, and the maiden rises and dips the hem of her robe into the stream of water, then walks around the bed, and placing her hand upon the head of the great hound, dips the hem of her robe into the blood. She approaches the thorn tree, and with her back to us, she wrings out the hem of her robe upon it. As she does so, the tree seems to stir and move, and tiny white buds and blossoms break forth from the tips of each branch. The hound stirs and licks his master's terrible wound; the maiden returns to her three-legged stool, and lifts up the knight's robe again. The sunlight fades slowly, and the blossoms close as shadow falls.

We know that it is time to leave, and as we step back from the bed, we see that a rough block of crystalline rock stands at its foot. There are faint letters cut into the rock, and we pause to read them before we leave the platform. [*A short pause here.*]

We walk back to the half-open door, and pass out of the hall between the great trees and the deep wells. The sun shines brightly over the dying orchard, and we see that some of the trees still bear healthy leaves and fruit buds. The sight of these trees gives us hope and knowledge of regeneration; we know that the secret lies in the mysteries that we have seen within the hall. As we consider these mysteries, we hear a rushing of wings, and a falcon flies down before us with his harsh cry. He turns his head from side to side, considering us with his bright, fierce eyes, and then leaps up into the cloudless sky. Higher and higher he flies, seeming to reach up for the sun itself: we follow the path of his flight until our eyes are blinded by the brightness and we can see no more . . .

Gradually we hear the sound of fast-flowing water, and as our sight recovers, we find that we are standing by a ford over a rushing stream. We stand upon a hard-beaten earth track, and know that behind us is the way to the walled city and high castle that we saw when we first met the heron, before our flight into the forest, the orchard and the purple hall. The secret of a cure for the wounded knight may be taught in that shining place: it is found deep in the wells that receive the blood and water from his wound.

We look across the stream, and see a shimmering mist, with a familiar scene beyond it. We wade into the waters, and feel them pull at our legs, but the stones of the ford are firm, and give us good footing. As we emerge from the stream, the landscape behind us fades slowly, and even the sound of rushing waters ceases. We find that we are back in the place where we started our journey, and we slowly open our eyes, returning to the outer world. As we do so, we hear faintly the chiming of a bell, and the falling of water into a deep, deep well. Now our journey to the hall in the forest is ended.

8

THE MYSTERIOUS ABBEY

Introduction

This visualisation combines two of the Five Mysteries: that of *The Son of Light* (represented by the ritual on page 143), and that of *The Vault* (represented by the visualisation of *The Hall in the Forest*, page 103). But it also fuses all Five Mysteries into one metaphysical or inner world structure: the inter-dimensional Cathedral that bridges many worlds, times and traditions.

The historical cathedrals, the great temples of the Middle Ages, remain something of an enigma to us. They reveal a technology and depth of skill that could not, truthfully, be matched or superseded today, yet they were built with the crudest hand tools. They also reveal many subtleties of design and technique in manufacture which give the lie to our modernist notion of progress and scientific development. Yet they were not ostensibly scientific ventures, they were declarations of religious vision. Furthermore it is startlingly clear to anyone with eyes to see that such structures intentionally merged pagan and Christian traditions and symbols, not merely in the sense of being located upon pagan sites, but as an organic and living combination of various streams of worship, belief and ceremonial practice.

There has long been a tendency to suggest that Christian propagandists adopted pagan symbols, deities and otherworld beings either (a) as a straightforward political statement of power or (b) in an attempt to obtain customers from among the obdurate pagan Saxons, Celts, Franks, Normans and other descendants of the early races of Europe. There is much truth in both of these suggestions, with ample evidence of policy from the writing of the early Church Fathers and later missionary saints. Yet such theories are not wholly satisfactory to anyone who has entered either the great cathedrals upon ancient power sites, or even remote country churches unspoilt by reformation or modernising. There was a period of time, perhaps no more than two or three centuries, in which pagan and Christian lore fused together: this was the same period which saw the building of the great abbeys.

Prior to this time there was still evangelising against directly pagan worshippers; the early churches, such as the Celtic Church which pre-dated that of Rome in Western Europe, had already been diminished through their unwillingness to be dominated politically or in terms of religious observance. The later developments of aggressive inquisition and then reformation were yet to come; but at the height of considerable unrest and extensive warfare, the vast cathedrals were raised and filled with symbols and structures ranging from the most recondite mathematics and metaphysics to anthropomorphic or theriomorphic carvings of entities that bridged Christian and pagan lore. The mystery of their presence increases the more we consider it. A tremendous eruption of power fused with expositional and magical skill and understanding caused these structures to be raised.

Today many of the cathedrals are in ruins, but their inner function remains active. To understand them we must transcend religious cults, and realise that they are universal vessels or thrones of spiritual energy. For many centuries there have been concise inner traditions of visualisation involving a mysterious Abbey. They begin to appear in literature in the Grail texts, along with otherworld castles: sometimes the castle and the church are one and the same building. But the composition of place, visualising an unusual and highly unorthodox cathedral (bearing in mind that most historical cathedrals abound in unorthodox material, even after reformation) was one of the inner teachings of heretical religious groups, magical orders and individual mystics or visionaries. It is upon this level, and within this enduring tradition, that we approach the Mysterious Abbey.

The basic pattern of a cathedral is that of the Six or Seven Directions (Above, Below, East, South, North, West and the seventh of the Centre or Within). The Six or Seven directions have always been part of the basic training of the magician, amplifying upon what may seem to be a very obvious – even crude – declaration of the human form standing upright upon the face of the earth. But this crude beginning has impressive developments in terms of stellar observation, astrology, astronomy and spatial or multi-dimensional mathematics. The Abbey, with a range of orthodox Christian correspondences developed out of the Directions, firstly declares this spatial relativity. Secondly, by its alignment, internal design, structure and mass, it shapes energy into very specific amplified patterns; these are intended to fuse with the human energies of the worshipping congregation, be they monastics or lay people. The building also may be read as a symbolic text, from shape, to divisions, to carvings, to stained glass. Finally it has an uplifting emotional and spiritual effect upon those within, due to the fusion of all of the foregoing, and the use of ritual techniques such as light, music, ceremonial services and so forth.

The Mysterious Abbey of our vision is what is rather grandly called a *consubstantial locus*, for it combines all worship sites and places in all worlds. Obviously we are only able to apprehend certain harmonic regions or aspects of this impossible truth: we begin with an Abbey; like many such buildings it may contain a stone circle or a pagan temple building; but it leads into many other worship sites (mainly non-Christian). Other beings, approaching from their own locii, will begin with the form familiar to themselves, and perhaps find The Abbey as an unusual variant. It is, in other words, the Western expression of an archetype of the *sacred space and form*.

We have the overt Mysteries of *The Son of Light*, in the form of the service conducted by the celebrants, and of *The Vault*, in the implication (in our variant) that a perpetual service is conducted, out of present reach, in the crypt. But the fundamental pattern of the Directions incorporates an entire cosmology and cosmography; it gives shape to spiritual and formless power.

The Mysterious Abbey

We see before us a framed picture of a simple landscape, of sparse green and brown moorland, with a track winding through it. The track is of beaten earth and rough stones, and is barely wide enough for two people to walk side by side.

We look closely at the frame for this picture; it is of dark-red metal, with deeply etched symbols around it. Two dragons make up the right- and left-hand side of the frame, their heads and tails reaching around the corners. The eyes of each dragon are of gemstones: one dragon has white eyes while the other has red. They chase each other around the frame, frozen for ever in perpetual motion.

As we look upon the frame with its etched dragons and strange hieroglyphs, the symbols seem to blur and move slightly, as if they had somehow been rewritten. With this blurring movement, the landscape suddenly becomes three-dimensional, and the picture frame opens out into a wide door framed by two massive carvings of dragons. We cross the threshold onto the earthen track.

We feel that we are upon high land; to our right we see the beginnings of fertile farmland, reaching away into wide, gentle valleys below. To our left the land rises, and in the distance there is a line of mountains capped with snow. The track before us runs through a fold in the sparse uplands, and we can feel a hint of frost in the air, despite the high, pale sun that shines upon our faces.

There is no sign of any animal or human life, although far below us in the valley we see smoke rising from the chimneys of a tiny farmstead. The land is silent, drawing in the faint sun of a midwinter noonday. Turning to look behind, we see two tall stone pillars, each carved with a spiralling serpent. The track passes through these pillars, and winds down to the valleys below. Standing by one of the pillars is a man in a blue-grey cloak and a wide-brimmed hat that puts his entire face into shadow. He carries what appears to be a tall shepherd's crook, though the end of the crook is carved into a dragon's head. As soon as we see him, he walks rapidly up the path towards us, and nods briefly in acknowledgement of our presence. He strikes the path with his crook, and heads off towards the distant fold in the land, where the path disappears out of sight. We may follow him if we choose, or return down the path to the lands below: but our quest is to find the mysterious Abbey which we know is somewhere in the hills ahead, so we follow.

Figure 14　The Mysterious Abbey

As we walk the road becomes steep, and cresting a hill, it drops through the fold that we could first see when we passed through the gate. Between two low ridges, it passes into a rocky area, where even the sparse moor grasses and heathers do not grow. We feel the hard, loose shale beneath us, and the sound of our passing echoes loudly from the ridges on either side of the path. Our guide turns to look back at us, and we realise that he moves without any sound, for his feet are bare.

A tumbled fall of large rocks obscures the track, but as we pass around these rocks, we find that we have entered a deep coombe or enclosed valley. Our guide has already stopped at the door of a small building, and waits for us. He stands before a low dome-shaped structure, roofed with turf on which tiny plants grow. The roof reaches almost to the ground, and we can see that the low walls are of dry stones, laid cunningly together without mortar. The door to this building is made of saplings woven together, and our guide pushes it open with his long staff, pressing against the wood with the dragon-carved crook. The door opens inwards, and our guide indicates that we should enter, though he himself remains outside.

We find ourselves in a small, low chamber, strewn with straw and dried herbs. There are stone seats built into the low wall, and a large fireplace at one end, with many more bundles of plants hanging around and within the chimney, which is built of large, uncut blocks of granite supported by a thick wooden beam. There is no one in the chamber, and our guide hooks the end of his staff around the door edge, and pulls it shut, leaving us in the shadow. We can hear no sound but the gentle moan of the wind in the chimney; the strong scent of dried herbs fills the little room, and nothing moves. We sit in the simple stone seats built around the wall, and meditate upon the peace and seclusion of this cell, considering why we have been brought here on our quest for the mysterious Abbey. [A silent pause here.]

As we meditate, we feel the temperature of the tiny chamber dropping, and realise that the afternoon must have passed, and that the sun is beginning to set. The light grows dim until we can hardly see; but in the dark fireplace a tiny ember glows, and we each take a handful of kindling from the pile beside the hearth, and placing this fuel upon the ember, we gently blow together, until our breath cause a flame to rise, and the fire springs into life. The light from the flames fills the chamber, and the odour of herbs becomes strong and heady. We lay some logs upon the fire, and sit absorbing heat and light. The air seems to fill with resinous smoke, and we feel strange movements around us, as if people were passing through the tiny room. Then the smoke clears, and standing before the fireplace is an aged woman, dressed in a plain dark robe. Her face is deeply lined and her hair is thin and white; in her withered hands she holds a distaff, upon which she seems to lean. She looks long and hard at our company, and as her gaze falls upon each of us, we feel fear, as if she looks into our deepest hidden hearts, and lays bare our follies and our shadows, judging us for what we truly are, and not what we wish to be, or might have been.

We sit very still, for this plain-looking crone radiates a terrifying power. She pulls a bundle of dried herbs from above the fireplace, and crumbles them upon the floor: with her distaff she draws a circle in the scattered leaves, and beckons us to look within it. We gaze into this circle, and the chamber seems to fade, the firelight shadows vanish, and we are gazing into a deep pool of night. Tiny stars shine within the depths, and we feel that we are gazing into a bottomless well of time and space. As the stars move, we see curious visions, and feel strange intimations which can hardly be expressed. [*A pause for meditation or vision is made here.*]

Now we seem to float within the immeasurable void, yet we neither move nor fall. The stars around us fade, until there is total darkness, and suddenly we feel the presence of the aged one who has brought us to this place that is no place. She asks us what we seek, what we would have her draw forth from the void, or where we would go within its endless weaving of space and time.

We consider the visions that have passed before us, and the insights that we were given in that moment of utter perception before the hearth: but we resolved before we began our journey that we would seek the mysterious Abbey, where all powers are joined in one holy communion. Even as we remember this resolve, the shadows begin to disperse, and we find that we are standing upon a broad, flat area, paved with square black and white stones. The black stones are utterly dark and shed no reflection, while the white stones glow faintly, as if they are made of polished glass or crystal.

Immediately before us rises the wall of a vast building, rising high above our heads, carved with many strange figures partly hidden in shade. A dim light illuminates the building from far above, and we realise that it is still night, and the stars spread their faint radiance over us. We slowly approach the building, and realise that it is a vast cathedral, like – yet unlike – those built in our own world. The central tower is high and square, a towering monolith above the walls and turrets that confront us. We realise that we are at the west end of the building, for a soaring archway frames double doors of black wood with ornate metal hinges and studs that shine as silver.

On either side of the door are carved figures, standing in niches: men, women, fabulous creatures, winged beings, animals, birds. Many are of creatures that we have never seen, yet others are of familiar legendary beings that we know of and have meditated upon. We consider this vast wall rising high above us and vanishing into the starlight. As we look up we lose sight of the carved figures and ornamental work, but we find a clear outline of turrets and tiny open archways near the rooftop, with stars shining through the pierced stonework. Briefly there seems to be movement high up, as if something is making its way across the roof: as we look it seems as if the air above is shimmering and flowing continually, though we cannot define what we see. We pause to consider the entrance to the Abbey.

The great double doors are firmly closed, and as we walk up to them, we realise that there is a small postern door within one of them. Upon this door is a plain ring, clearly set as a knocker. One of us goes forward to knock three times upon the door, but nothing happens. We draw close to this little door, waiting, feeling the carved figures around and above us, sensing the shimmering movement high upon the roof. There is silence, and we wait. [*A pause is made here.*] Just as it seems that we have knocked in vain, we hear a faint scraping sound, and the door opens before us: a faint light shines out, and there is a breath of warm, strangely scented air.

One by one we pass within, and find that it is held open by a man in a plain black robe and hood; he seems to be a monk, yet not of any order that we have previously encountered. He puts his finger to his lips in the sign of Silence, and beckons us to follow him. We find that we are in a porch or antechamber, and that the nave of the cathedral is beyond a high, carved and gilded screen. Our guide opens a curtained entrance in this screen, and we pass through. He remains behind, holding the curtain open. As we pass within we hear a faint resonant chanting, which seems to rise from the stone floor beneath us: a ritual is being celebrated in the crypt.

The cathedral is long and high, with many hanging lamps. There are no chairs, and the floor is marked with a curious red and green maze pattern that meanders between the pillars of the aisles; it shows the branches of a vast tree, gradually merging together into the trunk towards the centre of the building, and leading away to the east end. At the point of crossing there is no altar, but a soaring double arch (see Figure 15) which rises up to the roof. Looking down the long empty aisles, with the gold and silver hanging lamps and the bright colours of the mosaic maize upon the floor, our eyes are drawn upwards to this central double arch. We realise that it is in the semblance of two dragons coloured red and white, the red dragon inlaid with white markings, and the white dragon inlaid with red. The dragon's bodies cross in the centre of the double arch, and their necks and heads reach up. Looking upwards, we see that there is no ceiling beneath the tower, but that the roof opens through a circular hole, supported on either side by the jaws of the dragon arch, as if the dragons hold a great ring in their jaws. The immense length of the nave and height of the arch and tower draw us forward, and it seems as if we are always about to fall. [*A gong or deep bell is sounded seven times.*]

The sound of the deep chiming gong gathers our attention and the faint murmur of chanting below us grows louder. We see a figure below the soaring dragon arches, and he beckons to us. We walk slowly towards him, passing over the many branches of the great tree maze, and we see that he is robed in white and gold. This is the father abbot of the order, and as we approach him he makes a curious sign of blessing over our heads: his face is kindly and welcoming, yet we feel a deep current of power about and within him, and know that he is far more than a benevolent monk. He wears a white robe with a long golden cloak chased with many interwoven designs in silver, red and green. The patterns on the cloak seems to move and blur as he raises his hands to bless us. There is a rich, resinous smell of incense [*incense should be burned here if possible*] and the chanting wells up from directly below our feet to a harmonious ending.

In the sudden silence, we realise that we are standing directly beneath the double arch of the great dragons, reaching up into the deep tower. The father abbot lowers his arms, and looks upwards into the circle of black beyond the lamplight: we look also, and see deep within the darkness a tiny point of radiance. He bids us contemplate this primal light, and await the presence of the Son of Light who dwells within. [*Music may be played here, followed by a period of silent contemplation which is ended by the chiming of a bell.*]

With the chiming of a bell, we realise that the abbot has been

Figure 15 The Dragon Arch

celebrating a service while we have contemplated the mystery of the light: the abbey is filled with people, and the abbot holds his arms aloft, and from his hands a brilliant light fills the entire building. We look around us and see that to one side of the nave there are many men in dark robes, while to the other there are many women in light robes: we see faces that we know in their company, some that we suddenly remember for the first time: to each of us someone beckons, and we go to join their ranks, gazing upon the radiance that seems to float above the abbot. We sense a great presence, and the figure of the abbot seems to dissolve into light, and be replaced by another who opens his arms to us in perpetual blessing. The dragons of the double arch are filled with fiery light, and from their jaws fire runs around the great circle that they hold, leading into the depths of the tower above.

The two choirs of men and women begin to sing, and their voices merge into a strange chant that pulses with the radiance of the dragons. As they chant, a deep booming sound reverberates through the entire cathedral; the entire building rings like a bell or gong. For the first time we see beyond the dragon arch, and discover an array of other aisles, buildings, temples, worship places, rooms, chambers and open spaces under strange suns and coloured stars. All sacred places and temples converge upon this place.

As the chant rises, underpinned by the deep booming tone of the cathedral itself, rising from the crypt below, we feel drawn to leave the choirs and quietly make our way beyond the crossing, towards the east of the cathedral. The southern and northern transepts are hidden by tall screens, and when we reach the eastern portion of the building, we see that it has become once again a high-vaulted cathedral, and the countless other locations and places of power have vanished. At the eastern quarter is a plain altar carved of green stone, and beside it we see the brother who first welcomed us into the cathedral. He lays his finger on his lips in the ancient sign for silence, but as he does so we hear a still, quiet voice speak in our minds, saying that we may come again to the mysterious Abbey. There are many paths leading to it, and many experiences within it, and what we have experienced today is only a minute part of the truth and the Mystery.

The brother leads us behind the green stone altar, and lifts a trap-door in the floor: a crude ladder of wood lashed together with rope leads down into a chamber lit by smoking rushlights. The smoke is drawn away through small vents in the wall opposite, and from behind the wall we hear again the subterranean chant that we first heard on entering the abbey. There is no door, and we understand that this is a chamber where we may listen to the chant, but may not enter into the mysterious service that is undertaken within the crypt.

The voices chant without pause, in a deep droning sound interspersed with high fluting calls and cadences. As we listen to the chant the smoke from the rushlights increases, until the chamber becomes clouded and our vision blurred. [*Chanting here if possible.*] When our sight clears, the chanting sound has faded, and we find ourselves back in the rough stone hut where we first encountered the old woman and her circle of herbs. The fire is cold now, and the cold grey light of dawn passes in through the open door: our visit to the mysterious Abbey has lasted through a long winter's night.

We leave the stone hut, and make our way back down the track, which is now familiar to us. Out of the deep coombe, which has no other entrance or exit, and over the hill we walk, to see the sun rising before us. When we reach the pillars that mark the gate into the lower lands, the sun is already climbing into the sky, and touching the hard frost upon the moorland. We step between the pillars, and as we do so we hear the booming of a deep bell or gong, seeming to come from far away. On emerging from the gate, we find ourselves in a familiar room, and we sit in chairs set out for us.

Upon the wall is a picture of a landscape, in a metal frame made of two dragons with strange symbols etched upon it. We look at this picture, and see that it is of an abbey set within a steep mountain range, lit by a strange deep-blue light and many stars. The radiance of lamps shines from its arched windows, and a flame seems to flicker around the tall central tower. A narrow path leads right up to the abbey doors, and a tiny postern gate is open, with a small figure beckoning within it, seeming to welcome unseen travellers.

The image slowly fades, and then the frame itself disappears, leaving us to return to the outer world.

9

THE MYSTERY OF
MERLIN

The Merlin Visualisation

The story-teller opens the visualisation with the ritual Crossing Formula:

> In the name of the Star Father [*Height/Above*]
> The Earth Mother [*Depth/Below*]
> The True Taker [*Right Hand*]
> And the Great Giver, [*Left Hand*]
> One Being of Light. [*Totality/Circle*]

A small candle or nightlight is lit.

We begin by building in our inner vision the clear image of a narrow, winding track. This track leads up a steep hillside between overleaning trees and bushes; it is stony and rutted, and many wild plants grow around its steep banks. The trees curve over the track almost joining together above to create a tunnel. We enter into this living archway, and begin to climb up the hill. As we pass along the steep track, we can sense a presence in the bushes, watching us, following, sometimes moving ahead with faint rustling sounds. We can see nothing, yet we know that this presence, filled with curiosity, accompanies us on our journey.

The overgrown tunnel of trees ends at the top of the hill; we emerge onto a small, flat summit, and before us we see an immense view stretching away to the horizon. The other side of the hill leads down steeply to a wide, flat plain, lit by a deeper red sunset. The land is filled with long shadows and

low light, and far to the West there is a glimmer of sea. There
are low, rounded hills upon the plain, like islands, and as we
watch the sun set, tiny fires are lit on the summits, as the
watchers make ready for night. A bright star rises over the
horizon, radiating colour as she climbs into the dark-blue sky.

At the very edge of the treeline behind us is a ruined tower,
close to where we emerged from the steep path. The stones
are crumbling and black and green with age; long creepers and
ivy grow all over this tower, and its shape is softened by decay
and foliage. As we turn towards the tower, a light springs up
in the single window near the top, as if someone stands
unseen within the chamber and holds a lantern up for us.

We take one last look at the sunset lands far below, and turn
to enter the tower. There is a plain wooden door, charred with
fire and blackened with soot. We push upon it, but despite its
damaged appearance it holds firm and does not open.
Through the tangle of ivy high above our heads, a dim light
streams out of the slit window, but although we push on the
door and knock loudly with our fists, no one comes down to
greet us. We pause for a few moments to consider our
situation. [A short silent meditation here.] Out of the silence of
the night, we hear many tiny sounds: the rustle of wind in
leaves, the distant calling of an owl, and the faint lowing of a
cow far across the dark plain. Suddenly a shrill sound pierces
the night from the window above us, three high-pitched
whistling calls. From the bushes in the darkness we hear a
scurrying, scuffling sound, and the snapping of twigs as
something rushes towards us. For an instant we feel that a
vast creature is about to hurl itself into our midst, but to our
surprise it is a small black and brown pig that trots right up to
the door. The pig ignores us, and nudges at the foot of the
door with his snout, grunting and squealing in excitement. We
hear a loud click as if a lock has opened, and the pig pushes
the door open and runs inside. We hear him scrabbling up the
stairs, grunting happily. The door is open, and we hasten to
follow him.

The stairs are of crumbling, deeply worn stone, also
blackened by fire, and they curve steeply around the tower,
leading to a single chamber at the summit. We reach the
entrance, which is covered by a fine woven cloth with many
faint patterns upon it; the chamber within is perfectly round,
and lit by a small, dim lamp hanging from the centre of the
ceiling. A peat fire glows redly in the fireplace, and the floor of
the chamber seems to be covered with feathers. At first the
room appears to be empty, except for the pig, who is eating

Figure 16   Merlin's Esplumoir

noisily from a bowl by the fireside. Then we see a dim figure by the tiny slit window; he sits upon a three-legged chair, and has a hood drawn over his face. As we realise his presence, he sits up and takes notice of us, throwing back his dark hood. His face is lined and aged, his hair is long and silver-grey, he has a black and grey beard. His eyes are bright and penetrating, filled with compassion and understanding. He raises one hand and beckons to us slightly; we draw near and sit at his feet among the feathers on the floor. We know that this is Merlin, the Prophet and Master of the Western Mysteries. [*A silent pause for meditation here.*]

Merlin reaches into the shadows behind his three-legged chair, and as he turns we see that the chair legs each have a different colour, red, white and black, and are inscribed with minute curving, swirling patterns. His black robe flows over the seat of the chair onto the floor of the room. It has ragged edges, like crow feathers, and we can see the glimmer of other colours, revealed and then concealed, as if all the feathers of all the birds in the land are woven into another garment beneath. He turns back towards us, holding a large well-worn book, which he hold towards us so we can see it clearly. It has a scuffed, torn leather cover, with many stains, and is bound with blackened metal clasps and corners, which might be of silver. We can see faint words and decorations tooled into the aged leather, but the meaning is unclear. When he is sure that our full attention is upon the book, Merlin opens it, and turns the pages, seeking for a certain place. As the pages turn we hear faint sounds, of voices, music, chanting, animals running and calling, birds flying, and the distant, faint surging of waves upon the sea-shore. Merlin holds the pages flat, and the noises cease. He suddenly holds the great book up, with the pages open towards us, revealing what he has chosen.

We see black, curving script in neat lines, and a tiny illuminated picture in bright red, blue and gold marking the topmost left-hand corner of the page. It shows a walled, turreted city, and just outside the city gates, two boys playing with a ball. As we look at this tiny image, it expands and fills with sunlight. We seem to fall into the scene, and suddenly find ourselves standing before the tall, white towers and the wide-open gates, in the hot summer sunlight. We see that one of the boys is a child of almost ethereal grace and beauty, and know that this is the young Merlin; his companion is dark and haughty, and while the young Merlin wears a plain woollen tunic, faded and patched, his companion wears a rich black and gold tunic and green trews. They throw the ball to one another, and bounce it against the wall, but there is a tension in the game, as if they have just argued.

From the open gates a troop of soldiers strides; they are tall mercenaries in battered helmets, carrying an odd assortment of weapons. They are dressed in dull blue and grey tunics and trousers, with strips of brightly coloured rag and feathers in their long greasy hair and on their scarred arms. They suddenly surround the boy Merlin, and march off with him, down the road, away from the city. His companion stands aside, and bounces the ball, uncertain of what is happening. As the troop of mercenaries and the young Merlin pass down the long road, the light seems to fade, and darkness falls. We see his companion run into the city, and the gates are pulled shut. We feel sorrow, for we know that the young Merlin is to be imprisoned, and that someone intends him for a terrible death.

In the darkness, we hear the rustle of pages turning, and remember that we sit before the aged Merlin in his tower. He is leafing through a large leather-bound book, and somewhere in the chamber we can hear a pig snoring. Merlin selects a page, and once again holds it up for us too see; in the dim lamplight we see an illuminated picture of a hill. The side of the hill is cut away, in the manner of old pictures, to let us see within. Two tiny figures sit by the side of a pool deep within the hill; as we look at this scene, the image fills with light and expands; we somersault into the picture, and find ourselves upon our feet, behind a mound of fallen rock, littered with shovels, picks and buckets.

The pool is on the other side of the rocks, and we look over the mound to see the young Merlin, sitting cross-legged by the poolside. His eyes are closed, and he does not move; a faint light seems to radiate from him. Close by, sitting upon an ornate throne resting precariously in the mud and rocks, is a thin brooding man with long red hair and a wispy beard. He tugs at his lower lip with one hand, his fingers heavy with rings, many amulets and inscribed bands upon his arm. We realise that this is Vortigern, the great king. He stares at the waters of the pool, his heavy-lidded eyes occasionally turning to look at the boy. As they sit in silence, the waters of the pool begin to move and seethe; steam rises, and two shapes float to the surface, thrashing together in violent movement. The boy Merlin opens his eyes, and points triumphantly at the pool; we feel a sudden surge of joy and exaltation. There is an explosion of light so brilliant that our eyes close and fill with tears; vivid coloured shapes flash against our eyelids. Darkness falls, with tiny faint lights echoing and exploding within it.

In the silence that follows we know that the child was released from his imprisonment. We hear the turning of pages, and open our eyes to see the dim circular chamber lit by a central lamp. The fire glows and emits the distinctive smell of burning peat: a little pig sleeps before the hearth grunting softly. The aged Merlin pauses for a moment as he turns the pages, and smiles gently at an image which we cannot see. The air is filled momentarily with the rich scent of summer flowers, and for a moment he lingers over the page as if lost in memory. But he turns another page, and another more rapidly: faint sounds blur through the rustle of the turning pages, the galloping of horses, the clash of arms, the screaming of wounded men. Finally Merlin pauses in his turning, and holds the great book up for us to see, with the pages towards us. There is no written text, no tiny, formal, illuminated figures, but a deep window fills the double page, looking onto a dark-purple stormy sea. We are drawn through this window, and fall upon a cold sandy beach. The salt smell of seaweed is around us, and we hear the waves biting and lashing at the shore. A cold rain falls, and the wind swirls and screams.

Through the storms we hear the sound of wheels scraping through the wet sand and rocks; we see two figures, huddled against the weather, pushing a small cart. One wears a long dark cloak and a broad-brimmed hat; the other is dressed in a green and yellow chequered cloak, stained with rain. His long, flowing hair is bound by a silver circlet around his head, and across his back a small harp is slung in an ornate red and gold leather case. We realise that this is the bard Taliesin, Silver Brow, and that his companion is the mature Merlin. They trudge past us wheeling the cart, and we see upon it the body of a tall man wrapped in a bloodstained purple cloak. They pass very close to us, yet do not look at us; their faces are drawn, exhausted, sad.

By the shore they lower the shafts of the cart, and Merlin walks to the very edge of the sea. He faces into the storm, and raises his arms in supplication. His hat blows away in the rising wind, and we hear snatches of a deep, resonant chant in a language that we do not know. The storm builds, and the clouds lower slowly down upon the beach, issuing an endless flood of heavy rain. As we look at Merlin by the sea's edge, the waves washing over his legs, we realise that a dark shape is slowly approaching the shore: at first we think it is a

tall-necked creature from the deep sea, until we realise that it
is the prow of a boat. Standing in the stern is a huge figure
wrapped in undulating sea mist. We try to see more of this
mysterious vessel and ferryman, but at that moment the bard
Taliesin comes before us, and spreads out his tartan cloak, and
flings it over our heads. In the total blackness of that cloak we
see no more.

The sound of pages turning, and the dim red glow of a fire
bring us back to the tower; now Merlin shows us a series of
tiny images, rapidly turning the pages of the book with its face
towards us. we see men building a circular stone structure
with many doors and windows; a tall queen stands and directs
their work, while just upon the edge of each picture as it
ripples past, we see a naked man capering madly, wrapped in
ivy garlands and ropes of flowers, a set of antlers sprouting
from his hairy head. The building is finished, and a sudden
spiral of stars appears over it.

Merlin spreads the book upon his lap, where we cannot see
its contents, and turns to the last page. He pauses for a
moment, and slowly holds it up for us. We see the image of
the Weaver with her distaff, turning the Spindle of the Worlds
amid the depths of space and time. We see an aged man and a
tiny child, somehow both Merlin, yet sometimes becoming
female, now young, now old. We see ourselves there briefly,
then the image fades into a spiralling of stars, which slowly
turns and vanishes.

Merlin closes the book with a loud snap that jolts us wide
awake, and lets it fall heavily upon the floor, throwing up a
cloud of feathers. As the feathers fall we see a spiralling
pattern upon the back cover, embossed deeply into the leather
and coloured with many faded tints. It is a picture of an old
man with a tall staff walking along a spiralling road, leading to
the centre of the image where a tower is shown. The very top
of the tower is set with a rough white crystal. Merlin bends
and places both his hands over this crystal for a moment, and
we hear a muted resonance. He draws back and the crystal
seems to shine: we look within it and the embossed picture
upon the page turns black, until all we see is the crystal and
the images within it. [*A period of silent meditation here.*]

Now the image of the crystal fades slowly, and we look
about to find that we are in an empty chamber, with dawn
rising through a narrow window before us. The three-legged
chair is unoccupied, and we see that it is not coloured, as we
had thought, but of crude unpolished wood. The fire has gone
out, and the lamp is missing; but in the dusty feathers upon

the floor is a distinctive shape, as if a large book has lain there
for some time. The chamber has a faint odour of peat smoke,
and of pig.

We stand, and make our way down the spiralling stair
which seems to be very short, barely three turns; beyond the
door, which stands wide open, falling from its hinges with
age. The forest has grown right up around the tower. Indeed,
this seems almost a different tower and a different forest to
those which we entered, but a clear path leads away through
the trees, sloping gently downhill. It is as if the land has sunk
and the forest grown, and the tower crumbled into a tiny
overgrown stone chamber.

We take the path, and the sound of many birds singing fills
our hearts with joy. It is morning, and a new world comes
awake with the rising sun. [*Music here if possible, and a pause for
meditation and realisation.*]

Now our vision is drawing to an end; let us still our
awareness of the inner realms, and be wrapped in silence
before returning to the outer world. Now we close the way in
the words and by the power of the ancient Mystery: 'Peace is a
secret Unknown.'

*The word AMEN is resonated by all, and a period of silence observed.
The visualisation is now over, and those present depart in their own
time. The central light is left burning in the room.*

Analysis

The Method

This visualisation employs a slightly different method to our
other examples; it uses a ritualised opening and closing (though
this or similar openings may be added to any visualisation
sequence and such formal openings are quite commonly used
among established groups), and contains images taken from the
traditional life-story of Merlin. The method is to use a cycle or
sequence of encapsulated tales, generating brief key images into
any chosen Mystery (in this case the Mystery of Merlin), but not
expounding them in full.

Rather than intense visualisation upon a single theme, the
story-cycle, a method well established in oral tradition, particularly in the highly concentrated ballads and similar narrative
epics found worldwide, gives short, bright sequences of images

within an overall tale. Any one of these images may be a further tale in its own right, and in the almost lost art of true oral story-telling, many disgressive patterns and harmonic changes were commonplace. In oral tradition, the images may become rationalised or confused, though many of the magical ballads found in European and American tradition are remarkably coherent and powerful; but in magical practice we can employ the sequential process to create an overall change of consciousness. This change comes out of the totality of the sequence and its setting rather than from the intense employment of one major theme as in *The Hall in the Forest* (page 103) or *The Mysterious Abbey* (page 113).

Although the story-telling style may seem initially to be less intense than our other magical visualisations upon major themes, it is in many ways more demanding to undertake, for it involves a number of fairly rapid changes of imaginal scenery and locations, and a very wide range of energies. Rather than agonise over the technicalities of such a method, we allow the tradition or Mystery to work for us, for it has been tested through long periods of time, and has powerful innerworld connections. The images for our visualisation of Merlin are found in *The History of the Kings of Britain* and the *Vita Merlini*, expanded from oral bardic tradition by the twelfth-century chronicler Geoffrey of Monmouth. Such images are part of a mystical or magical tradition of story-telling containing both psychological and cosmological exposition. The visualisation does not extract these as academic texts, but employs the primary images found in the texts within an overall story in which we meet Merlin, who then reveals to us glimpses of the cycle of his Mystery, which is also in part his biography.

Background

The origins of this story-cycle are organic; they derive from a collective relationship between humans and the land, stretching back into the most primal prehistoric times. In its basic format, the Story tells of the First and Last Being – of his or her journey from divine childhood at the moment of creation of the worlds to ultimate old age and wisdom at the end of all things. This cycle is found in tarot, with the development of the Fool into the

Hermit, and in the major myth cycle of *Mabon* from Celtic tradition, though much of this cycle is now lost.[2]

It is also found in the Merlin literature, for in the *Prophecies* (preceded by some important biographical matter in the *History*) the child Merlin sees right to the end of time, often in remarkable detail in the context of British future history, but with a deeper cosmological vision of the powers of creation and destruction controlled by a Weaver Goddess, called Ariadne. In the *Vita* the mature Merlin experiences many transformative events and encounters, and finally retires to a stellar observatory with a small group of companions, having reached immense age and wisdom. The imprisoned child Mabon, in the *Mabinogion*, is only found through the assistance of the oldest creature of all – a salmon, totem beast of wisdom, who has heard him cry.

Thus the Mabon cycle, in which a marvellous child is stolen away from his mother at birth, kept prisoner in a mysterious place and is the subject of many heroic rescue ventures, is found inherent within the Merlin cycle, sharing many of the major characteristics, such as marvellous birth, cycles of experience, and immense antiquity. Both sets of tales include a strong emphasis upon the orders of creation; Mabon is found only with the assistance of many wise animals while the *Vita Merlini* has many totem animals in direct connection to Merlin, but also has an encyclopaedic expansion of natural history, added to the original oral theme by the prolific Geoffrey of Monmouth, who drew upon the classical sources known in his day. As the details of both the Merlin and Mabon Mysteries, and their close connections, have been discussed elsewhere[2] we do not need to take the comparison any further here. But there are some valuable teachings inherent in the theme which are relevant to advanced magical arts, particularly the motif of *imprisonment*.

The Merlin cycle reveals the child Merlin, born of human and non-human parents, imprisoned by the traitor Vortigern, who intends to sacrifice him in a corrupt magical ceremony to bolster up his own power. The prisoner is liberated through his prophetic revelations, which he makes in a cave beneath Vortigern's stronghold. The Mabon cycle reveals the mysterious child, stolen away from his mother at birth, imprisoned for an immense period of time in a fortress, but with many creatures and heroes attempting to set him free.

Similar imprisonment motifs are found in the Welsh *Triads* involving heroes, youths, and even King Arthur. This theme of Arthur and imprisonment is found in the important ancient Welsh poem *Preiddeu Annwm* in which Arthur and a band of heroes enter the UnderWorld. In the *Vita* the mature Merlin, in a state of madness, is imprisoned by King Rhydderch, chained to a post at the gates of the city. Their exchange of views is a typical allegorical argument between spiritual inspiration and worldly power. We find the theme recurring in a very widespread ballad, found in many variants in Europe and America, known in its English variants as *Lord Bateman* or *Young Beichan*. In this variant, the hero is chained to a tree or post by a Saracen king, but is eventually liberated by the king's daughter, who exchanges vows with the prisoner. Upon his departure, she seeks him out in a magical boat, an important recurring theme in Celtic legend, and eventually true love wins through.[4] Many further instances could be cited, relating to imprisonment with a magical or mythical significance.

It is generally assumed by commentators that the prisoner is in the UnderWorld or OtherWorld; many variants of the theme state this expressly and it is reiterated in the early Christian motif of Christ descending into the lower worlds to liberate the souls trapped therein. But here we find a paradox, for Christ also descended to the human world, and it seems likely that *this* world is the 'hell' from which we seek liberation. Gnostic tradition made no doubt about this teaching, but in magical arts we should always seek the primal foundation of any myth, no matter what tradition we employ in actual practice.

We can presume from the various traditions known, that the original tale concerned a divine child, Perfect Being, taken from his Mother, the Goddess, and imprisoned within, and through the creation of, the outer or expressed worlds. The vast cycle of time and adventures leading to his ultimate liberation comprises the story of the cycle of the worlds. When the Child is released, the worlds come to an end. But there is also the implication that the process is mirrored upon a human level, for the divine spirit is inherent within humanity: when the motif is attached to a human being, he or she undergoes a harmonic or parallel imprisonment . . . not merely that of physical incarnation, though incarnation is taught, significantly, in many spiritual traditions worldwide to be the route to liberation.

The imprisonment is within the UnderWorld, the region of direct power that underpins material dimensions, yet paradoxically contains the highest or originative spiritual reality. Thus a hero or otherwise sanctified person stands in for or reflects the Divine Child, in an experience which *mirrors* the primal myth. The true meaning of the enduring tradition of Sacred Kingship is found in this Mystery, far removed from the crude rationalisations of victimisation for the health of crops or any other superficial reductionist explanation.

Having said this much, there is no suggestion that *all* ritual sacrifices were undertaken with a profound purpose, for there is ignorance, viciousness and folly in all human activities at all times. We are referring to the deepest spiritual levels of the sacrificial motif, levels which have been claimed as the sole property of Christianity, but which are undoubtedly known in non-Christian and pre-Christian religions and metaphysical traditions.

A third resonance is found when the Divine Child, the Son of Light, incarnates within the human world. This is a reflection of the original imprisonment which occurred at the beginning of all worlds: but the Son of Light willingly imprisoned in the human world (a motif reflected yet again in his trial and death found in the redeemer myths) is really present in these worlds to liberate prisoners.

We find that Merlin, who begins as a magical child, is imprisoned by Vortigern: but his liberation is gained through the arousal of the Red and White Dragons, and he foresees to the very end of creation in his sequence of prophetic visions. The content of his prophetic vision contains keys to liberation, not only through prediction or fore-knowledge, but through the cosmological and magical visions within the text, which may be used as methods of transmuting consciousness.

The sacrificial element in the Merlin stories is found in the central motif of Threefold Death, which in the *Vita* is centred upon a youth, though in other variants is undergone by the prophet himself.[2] To conclude, the *Vita* Merlin lives to a great old age after many profound experiences, and withdraws to spiritual contemplation.

In magical traditions, he is still present in a dimension close to our own, and intimately linked to the land of Britain. We should state, however, that Merlin may be contacted without being in

Britain, and that there are many related images of innerworld teachers which will attune to the Mystery of Merlin, or to similar Mysteries within any specific land or location.

Contents of the Visualisation

Having summarised some of the essential background to the visualisation, we can now proceed to look at the contents. It is divided into twelve parts, and although these lead into one another within the overall frame of reference, they can be examined separately as follows:

1. Entry to inner world through the Crossing Formula and visualisation: concludes at the entrance to the tower, with a meditation period seeking admission.
2. Appearance of totem beast who gains admission which was previously barred.
3. Ascent of tower and vision of the aged Merlin concluding with meditation upon his presence.
4. The magical implements: three-legged chair and book. These are the traditional implements of seership and prophecy. The ancient seeresses of classical Greek and Roman temples or oracular shrines sat upon tripods; the triple symbol is preserved in legend and folklore, relating to the three aspects of the Great Goddess, or the three essential ingredients or magical compounds of Blood, Sweat (Seed), and Body. In metaphysics these are the triple universal threads of Time, Space and Energy, woven inseparably by the Weaver. The three strands or tripod legs are coloured red, white and black. Symbolism of this sort was used very specifically in alchemy for certain materials, prior to the invention of standard tables of reference.

The Book may be regarded in several different ways: it is a formal presentation of the Mirror or Shield of the Northern Quarter, the reflecting and purifying Element of form, or Earth. It is the book of all knowledge and wisdom, but in this particular case it is the book of the Mystery of Merlin. This is the inner or magical version of that 'Great Book' which Geoffrey of Monmouth claimed to have used to copy his *History*; it is the volume of collective and ancestral memory and myth. It may only be activated, however, in very specific modes or levels, for a total activation would lead to madness and destruction of the persona.
5. Image (a): The young Merlin and his companion or twin (tanist) playing ball outside the city. Although this refers directly to the legend of Vortigern and Merlin, and the Saxon mercenaries

and invaders, there are some sub-textual elements worth commenting upon briefly. *Two Youths*: this relates to the ancient pattern of sacred kingship, in which two brothers or polarised male candidates were frequently found. They become the Dark and Light Brother in myth or folklore, the Accuser and the Innocent. We find this in the Christian mythology of Jesus and Judas, but the motif is widespread in legends of a non-Christian origin or tradition. In the Mystery of Merlin they are Merlin and Dinabutius; Merlin is accused of having no proper father in a childish argument, but this reveals his double nature (born of virgin and daemon) to the messengers of King Vortigern. Finally Merlin is carried off to be sacrificed, in order that Vortigern's false tower might be upheld by innocent blood. Thus this earliest reference to the youthful Merlin (from the *History*) is an undoubted sub-story linked to the pagan system of sacrificial kingship. It ends with a feeling of sorrow, loss and imprisonment.

6. Image (b): Young Merlin and Vortigern at the underground pool. Merlin proves that two dragons exist, and their appearance leads him into a prophetic trance. The vision ends with a feeling of joy and liberation. We do not, however, enter into the prophetic sequence at this stage.

7. Merlin examines his personal life in the book, but does not reveal it to us as a specific vision.

8. Image (c): The carrying of the wounded king to the Other-World. This is a major visualisation in its own right, but here we only enter into part of it, and that part is shrouded in mystery and uncertainty. The bard Taliesin protects us from the presence upon the boat that Merlin has summoned: if we saw this Ferryman direct we would die. In visualisations he is usually given the form of Barinthus, a type of sea or navigating deity, as named by Geoffrey in the *Vita*. In the present vision, however, he appears in a higher or more direct form.

9. Image sequence (d): A rapid series of pictures blurring together, showing the mad Merlin and his sister Ganieda, who is an archetypical human embodying the goddess Briggidda/Minerva, building their stellar observatory.

10. Image (e): The Weaver (the trump of Judgement in the Merlin Tarot). This major Image is the culmination of the sequence that we have seen. There are a number of implications concerning sacred kingship, wounding, imprisonment and liberation, and the synchronicity or spiritual astrology of such events through long spirals of outer time (not necessarily cognate with modern astrology).

11. The back of the book: shows Merlin climbing to his tower or *esplumoir* to await our coming. The final paradox is in the crystal of vision set into the image of the tower on the back cover of the great book. It is at this point that we may receive visual impressions from other worlds and beings; these are not necessarily conditioned by the imagery built up through the story sequence, and in practice may contain many surprising elements.
12. Conclusion: transformation of chair, absence of book and lamp. Merlin has departed, and the magical implements of book and three-legged chair plus the lamp (symbol of The Hermit in tarot) have vanished. The chair that remains has no magical qualities, and we are left to decide for ourselves regarding the truth of the experience of meeting Merlin. The tower and landscape, however, are transformed, as if a long period of time had passed, far longer than the one night implied by the sequence of vision and the rising dawn. If Merlin revealed the mythic past to us, this last phase of the visualisation is the paradisal future. We meditate upon this transformative possibility, as we return to the present time and place.

Finally the sequence is closed by a period of silent meditation on the word of power, *Amen.*

10

THE RITUAL OF THE SON OF LIGHT

Introduction

The following ceremony is based upon an invocation which contains elements held in common by pagan and early Christian religion, mysticism and metaphysics. Similar invocations were preserved in oral tradition in Gaelic-speaking regions of Ireland and Scotland for many centuries: such traditional prayers or ceremonies represent the collective consciousness fusing pagan and Celtic or primal Christian beliefs. Upon this level of the imagination, there is no hostile separation between the new religion and ancient custom or worship; here we encounter Christianity in a primal state, before the propagandising of later political manipulators. This level is often called 'Celtic Christianity' in modern literature and discussion, but to label it as such is a gross over-simplification. We need only consider the great Celtic saints such as Columba to discover that they evangelised against paganism; but the Celtic Church was in turn suppressed by the developing Roman Church, and eventually vanished.

Whatever the truth of this complex organic situation of development, a truth which is not accessible to rational historical research, there seems to be an accord between the primal elements of Christianity and the fundamental beliefs of paganism, particularly in the philosophy of the Druids and certain related aspects of Greek mythology and worship. This does not imply that the practices, rituals, gods and goddesses of paganism were necessarily acceptable to the evangelising early

Christians (for we know that they were not), but that the ancient world recognised harmony of concepts, relationships between deep levels of belief and metaphysics. Thus pagan culture was in many ways more tolerant than the political Christianity that developed after the fifth century, in which differing beliefs were seen as rivals rather that potential allies in the quest for a relationship between humanity and divinity. This expansive attitude is still preserved, to a certain extent, in the East today, though we should be cautious about generalising when comparing cultures in the modern world with those of the past.

Elements of harmony and fusion between cults are particularly important in magical arts, and act as anchoring points for the construction of rituals and visualisations that seek to develop new approaches and techniques. This has regrettably become hopelessly confused with a type of intellectual theosophy or pantheism that correlates all symbols, powers, deities and beliefs into neat, arid lists. Alternatively we have the vagueness of 'New Age' 'spirituality' – cosy, loving and bland. One method of answering this problem may be found through dedicated magical work, for if we resist the temptation to be academically rigorously comprehensive (which invariably means spending one's energy playing with words rather than seriously entering upon the magical disciplines described by the words) we may move to deeper levels of consciousness. Providing we do not swing to the other extreme, of cuddly pan-cultural lovingness and mock-spirituality, we may gain some interesting material from our efforts.

There are generic rituals and visualisations that arise through focusing consciousness upon the harmonic areas of imagery and power, shared between the early religions. The fusion of Celtic Druidism, which absorbed many potent chthonic magical practices from older religions, with primal Christianity, which acted as a channel to a specific spiritual power, is particularly fruitful. In this context of fusion, we may use the *Ritual of the Son of Light* as a wholly Christian, wholly pagan, or mutual ceremony. It is in this last role, in which pagan Mysteries and primal Christian spiritual symbolism and power merge together, that the ceremonies are at their most effective.

The basic ceremony is short, and may be worked effectively by one person: a group of celebrants may work with any number by simply allocating roles, as all officers are of equal significance. When there are more than five officers, however, it is necessary to harmonise the group by allocating members to specific quarters and cross-quarters (see Figure 17).

Another very effective method which has been employed in a number of modern ritual workings is to allocate an immediate polar partner to each officer such as a member of the opposite sex who acts as a reflector or joint mediator in the same Quarter. This role is not identical to that of the polar mediator in the opposite Quarter (such as, in our ritual example, a goddess-form in the North opposite a god-form in the South). Supporting partners may use imagery from the mythos or structure connected to the main officer: there are many associations found in myth and legend in which a figure has companions, assistants or counterparts.

If there are sufficient people present, each officer can work a triadic pattern: the active celebrants (with the lines to speak) and two supporting officers on his/her right and left. It is also possible to sub-divide the text into lines allocated to the polar or supporting officers if this method of working is preferred, though it is important not to weaken the effect of invocations by dividing them into too many tiny performance units without flow and coherence.

The Role of Mediator

The fifth officer, termed the Mediator in this text simply because of our emphasis upon mediation in advanced magical arts rather than because of any formal name or title, is symbolised by the implement of the Cord. This is the fifth Element or Ring, sometimes called Ether, or more simply Spirit, or Truth. The Cord is the only implement which can connect the Sword, Rod, Cup, and Shield or Mirror by a variety of *patterns*. In very simple magical arts, the Cord is the sole implement carried by the magician when all others need to be hidden or are, in more modern contexts, impractical for various reasons. The Cord is the linking or mediating line between the worlds, one of the strands in the fabric created by the Weaver (see page 90). To make a ceremony of this sort fully effective, it should be undertaken with each officer working as the mediator in turn: thus with a group of five people a full cycle of the ritual would

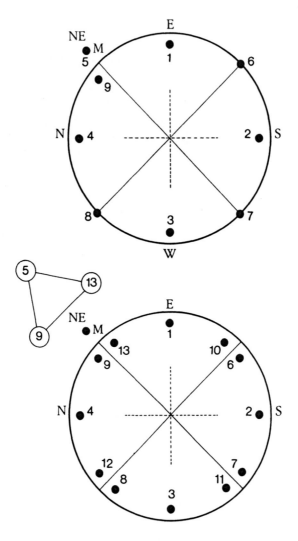

Figure 17   *Officers in the Circle showing Five-Thirteen Stations*

E: East   S: South   W: West   N: North   M: Mediator

require five workings. The nature of magic is such that this cyclical celebration will result in a considerable amplification and acceleration of energies.

Although the Mediator is placed in the North-East, the point of spiralling transition between each turning of the Wheel or Circle, a single magician may work the ritual in a fivefold cycle by undertaking the mediation to each quarter in turn, then at the centre for the fifth and culminating ceremony. The time taken between workings is not crucial for a group, but for the individual there should not be too long a period between each working of a Quarter. In either case a very long interval will run the risk of dissipation of energy and concentration, though practised magicians can and do meet up only once a year or even less frequently, and still work with efficiency.

Obvious calendar correlations are those of the Four Seasons, with the fifth rite worked at the turning-point or cross Quarter of early February (Candlemass being an important festival shared by pagans and Christians alike). Alternatively the phases of the Moon could be employed, with the fifth and final working coming on the second new moon (East: New Moon/ South: Full/ West: Waning/ North: Dark). No matter how the group develops the ritual pattern, it is important that all members conduct the mediation in rotation: there are no star performers in advanced magical arts, and no 'senior' members of an advanced magical circle. This does not, incidentally, imply any kind of contrived egalitarianism or politicised system; in modern magical terms it is merely common sense to have all members of a group developing and working as equally as possible.

While we have discussed, elsewhere in this book, the concept of balanced specialisation which was widely employed in ancient Mysteries and magical orders or religious communities, be they pagan or Christian, this group method becomes increasingly difficult and potentially dangerous in the twentieth and twenty-first centuries. Limited specialists tend to be weak links in a group for any human activity, and we are now experiencing the devastating result of over-specialisation in materialist sciences. In spiritual terms the rotation of the mediating role is an acknowledgement of our inner potential; in tarot symbology it is represented by the trump of The Fool who transforms into all other trumps in a cycle of adventures and development.[3]

The 'Z' Pattern

The 'Z' or Lightning or Undulating Sign plays a major part in the Western Mysteries, though it has various forms in expression and published theory. The glyph may be used very effectively as an overall pattern for the *Ritual of the Son of Light*, in which the cycle of Fivefold Mediation described above is specificially orientated. A full fivefold cycle of the ritual requires each officer of a Quarter to be Mediator in turn in the following sequence (rather than around the Circle in the customary rotation): 1 East; 2 South; 3 North; 4 West; 5 Centre. The *directional* emphasis is very important in magic generally, though it is usually confined solely to the simple concepts of the Quarters. Alternatively we find it expanded into intellectually complex structures that seem very satisfactory and thorough on paper, but may become impractical in actual ceremonial work. The actual rhythm and flow of energies generated by the 'Z' patterns is one of inner teachings of the Mysteries, a spiritual pattern that cuts across all regular cycles in all worlds. We shall encounter it in a direct ceremonial form in the *Weaving Ritual* (Chapter 13).

Expanding the Ceremony

There are a number of areas that may be opened out as specific invocations, visualisations and aspects of the main ceremony. Examples of such expansions are given separately, and can be used where indicated by the line numbers in the main text. Key identity lines for the Four Quarters, such as 'I am a Light and a Keeper of Lights' (**South**, part 5) are major phrases or *words of power*, if we may use the term, from individual ceremonies and sophisticated ritual observances and inner traditions associated with the Four Directions. In a fully operational and regularly observed Mystery or cycle of rituals, an entire ceremonial system would be developed from such key phrases. In magical work, the use of such key phrases, or chants, calls, words of power, and similar units of empowered or concentrated consciousness, taps into enduring energies and inner traditions behind the ceremony.

We might visualise, for example, a line of contact with imaginative and historical orders or traditions who upheld certain truths through their beliefs and practices, and who exist upon inner transpersonal levels of altered consciousness beyond serial time. This concept is found in the expansion text for the **South** (part 5.(a)), and is well known in one branch of mystical and magical initiation with a very long history in the form of *The Order of Melchizadek*, though this term is only one ostensible analogy or name (based upon biblical references) for a spiritual reality that transcends orthodox religion or sectarianism.

All of the foregoing, however, is a side issue; the main objective is the invocation and presence of the Son of Light. This objective is balanced by the second half of the ceremony in which the energies aroused are sent forth, usually with a specific purpose in mind, which has been formally defined before the ritual commences. As there are a number of technical matters that might be of interest in our context of advanced magical arts, a short analysis of the ritual from the inner operational viewpoint is given after the working text and expansions. It should be stressed that the analysis offered is only part of the complex content of the ceremony: here we have a typical example of a ritual which is exoterically or outwardly simple and direct, but esoterically or inwardly full of many subtleties and ramifications. A typical task in long-term magical training and work would be to keep a journal of results from this ceremony, and to occasionally expand the analysis according to the effect of the rituals and associated insights gained during the periods of meditation. Such diaries are only valuable, however, when they are not obsessive or time-consuming.

The Ritual Text

(May be undertaken with any number of officers or as a ceremony for one person. The text which follows assumes a minimum of five officers.)

OFFICERS

1. **East**; 2. **South**; 3. **West**; 4. **North**; 5. **Mediator**.

The ceremony begins in darkness with all participants except the mediator standing in their allocated position around the Quarters of the Circle. (See Figure 17.) The Mediator sits in the North-East.

1. [**East** *strikes a gong three times and says:*]

Peace is a Secret Unknown.

2. [*All celebrants chant a resonant AMEN.*]

3. [*A period of silent contemplation, stilling of energies, and seeking the condition of inner peace.*]

4. [**East** *positioned before a simple altar in the East: lights a taper, and lights the Eastern lamp with the following words:*]

Let there be a light uttered from the void. Peace to all Signs and Shadows, Light in all ways of Darkness, and the Living Son of Light reborn for ever. By the power of Life vested within me blessed be this Eastern Gate and blessed be the Element of Air. [*Makes sign over the Eastern flame, and opens Gate of the East. Hands lighted taper to* **South**.]

5. [**South** *faces Southern Quarter and lights the lamp positioned there.*]

Let there be a light increasing and illuminating in the South. I am a Light and a Keeper of Lights: blessed be this Southern Gate and blessed be the Element of Fire. [*Makes sign over the Southern Flame and opens Gate of the South. Hands lighted taper to* West.]

6. **West** *faces Western Quarter and lights the lamp positioned there.*]

Let there be a light radiating in the West: by the power of Love vested within me blessed be this Western Gate and blessed be the Element of Water. [*Makes sign, etc.*]

7. **North** *faces Northern Quarter and lights the lamp.*]

Let there be a light reflecting in the North: by the power of Law vested in me blessed be this Northern Gate and Blessed be the Element of Earth. [*Makes sign, etc.*]

8. *Mediator remains seated.*

Let these powers be at one.

[*All chant a resonant AMEN.*]

[**East** *strikes gong three times.*]

Expansion of Ritual (1) Celtic archetypes and god-forms.
(May be omitted, in which case the ceremony moves direct to part 9.)

Parts 4–8 are first completed, and the ceremony returns its focus to the
East:

4.(a) **East:** I call upon the great power of the Lord of Life, who
roars as a whirlwind and summons all living creatures to his
court. Behold him now in his Image of Cernunnos, crowned
with the noble spreading antlers of the stag, robed in the
glory of flames and of living green. He enters through the
Eastern Gate at Dawn: his companions are the grey Wolf, the
gentle Deer, the black Crow, and the soaring Eagle, king of
Air. As Guardian of the Gates he opens now the Way of Life
and fills the Circle with his blessing, his power, and the
unseen presence of the One Being whom he serves. [*Blows
three times upon a horn/ or utters the Call of Air.*]

5.(a) **South:** I call upon the ascended Lord of Light, who shines
victorious and beautiful as the sun, and brings all souls of
light together in one convocation. Behold him now in the
Image of Belenos, crowned with radiant Fire, robed in gold
and white and deep blood-red. He enters through the
Southern Gate at Noon riding on a pure-white Mare: he bears
the spear of perfect balance pointed to the stars, and leads a
company of kings and queens, priests and priestesses of
eternal Light. As Guardian of the Perpetual Assembly in the
inner City of Light he opens now the Way and fills the Circle
with his blessing, his power, and the unseen presence of the
One Being whom he serves. [*Sounds a high-toned bell three
times/or utters the Call of Fire.*]

6.(a) **West:** I call upon the Lady of perfect Love who purifies the
seas in which the worlds are born, and brings to flood and
ebb the rivers flowing beneath all manifest being. Behold her
now in her Image of Briggidda, crowned with the deepest
glory of the sunset, robed in blue and green and silver. She
enters through the Western Gate at Evening and a radiant
star shines upon her brow: her companion is a Dun Cow
carrying upon her back a deep copper cauldron with a crystal
rim. As Guardian of the Blessed Isles she opens now the Way
and fills the Circle with her blessing, her power, and the
unseen presence of the One Being whom she serves. [*Sounds
three chimes upon a bowl or resonant glass vessel/ or utters the Call
of Water.*]

7.(a) **North:** I call upon the Lady of Universal Law who sets the stars in motion upon the endless mirror of night. Behold her now in her Image of Arianrhota, Lady of the Silver Wheel, crowned with silver and crystal, robed in deepest black. She enters through the Northern Gate at Midnight and holds up a dark mirror for any who dares look within. Her companions are the Bear, the Owl, and the tiny Wren. As Guardian of the Deepest Mysteries of Death and Birth she opens now the Way, and fills the Circle with her blessing, her power, and the unseen presence of the One Being whom she serves. [*Sounds three times upon a deep gong or very resonant low-pitched drum/ or utters the Call of Earth.*]

The ceremony now moves to part 9 of the basic text and proceeds into the Mediation of the Son of Light.

9. **Mediator** *stands and faces* **East** *in position of invocation.*

In the Name of the Son of Light The Son of Maria,
Foster son of Briggidda in Avalon
Keystone of the Arch of Heaven,
Who joins as one the forks upholding of the sky.
His the Right Hand.

[*Lights right-hand pillar flame before the Eastern altar.*]

His the Left Hand.

[*Lights left-hand pillar.*]

His the Rainbow Letters all in rich fermented milk.

[*Makes archway sign over the pillar flame, linking them together and opening the Gate of Light.*]

We shall go in his Name, in all shapes of shapes
   in all colours of colours, upon the Path to Peace.

[*Processes around the circle with lighted taper. The Four Officers join the circling, and eventually all other celebrants if possible.*]

Do you see us here, oh Son of Light?
Says the Son of Light *I see.*

[*Celebrants return to their positions.*]

10. [**East** *strikes gong three times: all meditate upon the Son of Light.*]

(*See operating notes for potential of this meditation and roles of each officer.*)

11. **East:** Blessed be the Light that comes among us.

South: Blessed be the Light that lives within us.

West: Blessed be our Being One in Light.

North: As One Body in All Worlds.

All chant AMEN.

12. **Mediator:** Let us radiate the Light in the Name of the Son of Light according to our dedication and purpose.

North: By the power of the Wheel of Stars at midnight I transform, send forth, and remain at Peace.

South: By the power of the Radiant Sun at noon, I transform, send forth, and remain at Peace.

West: By the power of the setting Sun and rising Moon at evening I transform, send forth, and remain at Peace.

East: By the power of the rising Sun and Morning Star I transform, send forth, and remain at peace.

Mediator: Peace to all signs and shadows, light in all ways of darkness, and the Living Son of Light reborn for ever.

13. [*Mediator may light a central lamp from the Eastern flame to act as a focus for meditation or dedication if required.*

The Four Quarter Lights are extinguished and closing signs made during the above ritual operations and phrases. A gong is chimed at the closing of each Quarter.

All celebrants depart in silence. Alternatively a period of contemplation of the central Light, and departure at will. The central light is left burning.]

Commentary upon the Ceremony

(Refer to main text and expansion text as indicated.)

The ceremony is designed for five people, acting as officers in each role in a fivefold cycle, though it may be undertaken by one individual or a larger number (see Introduction to the ritual). This corresponds to the Fivefold Pattern found in magical traditions, in which the Four Powers or Elements are unified and transformed by a Fifth Power. The Fifth may be either the original seed of all Being, or the sum of the Four. This is the mystery found in Kabbalistic mysticism in which the Kingdom or outer world is affirmed to be identical to the Crown, or originative Spirit.

Beginning in darkness: a ritual enactment of the unknown and unknowable Void from which Being is breathed forth. The officers approach this state of Non-Being through internal stillness and suspension of directed consciousness.

1. *Three gong resonances* affirm the three supernal or ultimate conditions of Energy (Consciousness), Time and Space. Accompanied by spirit-breath or summoning of the Inner Fire from the Void (all officers emerging from formless contemplation) to generate the first phase of the field of power focused within the Circle.

'Peace is a Secret Unknown.' This ritual phrase is the last line of a stilling or de-patterning ritual and meditation, connected to the Mystery of the Weaver Goddess (see page 90). The phrase is employed in regular meditation, and is similar in operation to the *mantrams* of Eastern mysticism. Although it is not possible to give a proper insight into its power through a written interpretation, we might approach it as follows:
Peace is the original non-condition of Non-Being, or Stillness. To the heavily conditioned, coagulated, outward-seeking consciousness, Peace is an unattainable state, briefly touched upon only at the moment of physical death. During esoteric disciplines, the so-called secrets of transcendent consciousness or the inner worlds are gradually revealed and understood; these are merely a sequence of initiations or growth towards the unattainable condition of Perfect Peace. But true spiritual consciousness reaches beyond the secrets to one unified Secret, comprehended only in an altered state of awareness. Ultimately even this secret of secrets or unity with spiritual Being is dissolved, towards a non-condition or non-Being. Thus Peace is a Secret Unknown.
The associated technique consists of suspension of consciousness through a deep realisation of the concepts of Peace and Knowing: the two concepts (which are human conscious analogues of higher modes of universal consciousness/energy) mutually dissolve one another. In simpler terms, the act of

unknowing a secret at the deepest levels of consciousness leads us to a state beyond consciousness and before Being. This state is unattainable, but the key phrase acknowledges the truth of unattainability, for peace is a secret unknown.

2. AMEN is chanted as a long, resonant humming or Word of Power. This chant gives shape to the energies now flowing through the Circle, energies which are deconditioned from their normal cycles through the stilled consciousness of the officers, and are liberated through the spirit-breath which hovers over the unknowable point or condition of Peace.

AMEN is a *Mother Word*, the resonance of the supernal powers (the supernal Triad of Crown, Wisdom and Understanding upon the Tree of Life). When elongated in chant form, AMEN contains all four vowels (AOMIEN) and two unifying matrix resonances (*M* and *N*). There are several ways of interpreting the sound, but all derive from the concept of a spiritual resonance or Word that utters forth the ground of all being, and resounds through all Worlds. The vowels are utterances of the Four Powers or Elements, while *M* and *N* are sigils of power in their own right.

M is the Mother Wave or undulating consciousness within the deep of Being, Space and Time. It also shows as a glyph the important metaphysical *pentad* found upon the Tree of Life (see Figure 3 and meditate upon the relationships developed through Spheres 2/3/4/5/6 and 4/5/6/7/8). A further set of pentads of great meditational value is found by examining the relationship between the higher Spheres and the Bridge across the Abyss. (*Daath* in Hebrew mysticism). All of these concepts are shown and uttered in the Mother Word or Sigil *M*.

N is the second undulating or wave-form of universal Being. It is the 'Z' or 'N' sign of Lightning, a serpentine or zig-zag path that cuts across the universal ground of Being. It is especially associated with the Son of Light, a spiritual force that liberates, redeems and obviates all cycles and conditions. It is, significantly, the sigil of the Hanged Man[3] who redeems or transforms all states of Being by taking a Secret Path across the Abyss and mediating divinity directly to humanity.

Thus the Word of Power comprises the Four Elements, the Mother Goddess, Her Son, and of course the unifying entity of their entire Being, the seed and sum of All.

3. *Inner Peace.* After the utterance of the Word of Power, the energies are once again stilled (as above), but not dissolved or closed down. This period of still meditation is preparatory to the lighting of a flame which brings the spiritual power as a real identity and presence within the prepared field of ritual, which is, of course, the magical Circle on one level, and the consciousness and physical form of the ritualists, both collectively and individually, upon another.

4. **East** *Let there be, etc.* The Eastern officer reiterates the creation process of Being out of Non-being, now reflected as Light out of Darkness. Drawing upon the undeniable power of Life within his/herself, the officer lights a flame which is unified with an inner universal life energy. The officer attunes this force to the concept and power of Air, the first of the Four Original Powers. He/she visualises as strongly as possible the attributes of the Eastern Quarter, drawing upon the worlds, orders of beings, implements, and imagery as required. The subsequent specific invocation, however, is *not* pre-empted (see expansion text) for this initial Opening of the Quarters is the first cycle of assembling the magical Circle through its primal Elemental Powers.

The major telesmatic Images or divine entities are not invoked until the Circle is fully alive and balanced; in old-fashioned parlance we might say they could appear in their negative aspect or demonic shadow if invoked without proper training, preparation and actual balanced conditions within the ritual working of the moment. This crucial concept is merely an amplification of a general condition and should not be taken as propaganda concerning 'evil' in ritual magic. In other words, if an unfit person tries a strenuous sport, he or she may suffer injury: anyone jumping from a plane without a parachute is likely to be killed; a fine racing car cannot travel at speed over rough terrain, and so forth. That which is valid and meaningful in its proper context is equally dangerous and destructive out of context.

5. **South** *receives light from East.* The procedure outlined above is repeated by the officer for each Quarter, according to the attributes and forces inherent within that Quarter. The phrase *I am a light and a keeper of lights* is a line from a Mystery ritual

known as *The Mask of the Bright One*, and is a typical example of a line or phrase or word acting as a power matrix. We shall encounter this cross-reference and key attuning in the expansion and invocation of the South, in which the god-form invoked is visualised as wearing a mask. The entire Mystery ritual, however, is not included, as it is a separate ceremony and separate specialised magical art. The key phrases for **West** and **North** are replaced by the much-used and little-understood ritual line *'by the power vested in me . . . '*. While making such a declaration the ritual officer must for a timeless moment (brief in outer duration) mediate utterly the Power of Life, Light, Love or Law. Note that the Elemental Power (Air, Fire, Water or Earth) and the Gates are blessed but not mediated through the human officer. The power mediated may transform and resolve or redeem the Elements, but the Elements cannot of their own accord transform or redeem a human soul.

The entire format of opening Gates and setting signs upon them, is a matter of *tuning*. There is no room in advanced magical arts for idle superstition: we are not, for example, vaguely hoping that some higher power will protect us against ravening phantoms (no such entity could enter or exist within a properly attuned Circle, as it would be dissolved into its constituent elements and cease to reflect upon itself). Although the concept of tuning has many analogies to modern technology, it is a tuning of *consciousness, living energies, and conceptual or imaginal matrices* and not of mechanistic or electronic components.

8. By part eight of the ceremony, the Four Powers and Elements are activated and set into balanced resonance or motion. This tuning of life forces and inner dimensions is then unified through the Mediator, who visualises their harmonious fusion and interrelationship, while the Four officers mediate the forces which they represent. The second AMEN is uttered, at which point all officers visualise the unification and perfect balance of the Powers.

With this second AMEN and the fusion of vision and energies, the Circle is turned, so to speak, into a higher spiral, octave and dimension. Its rate of spin or of power, is doubled. If we consider a flat map, the cycle has turned through all four phases, and now crosses the North-East into a new status. If we see it as spiral, the spiral turns and the assembled forces and consciousness move onto the next level of the spiralling path. If we see it as a sphere of energies, the entire sphere is modulated through an octave of frequency or consciousness. In terms of the Tree of Life or Three Worlds, we pass from the Lunar World (the Spheres 10, 9, 8, 7 or planetary forces of Earth, Moon, Mercury and Venus) into the Solar World (Spheres 7, 8, 6, 5, 4 or planetary forces of Venus, Mercury, Sun, Mars and Jupiter). We move the assembled consciousness of Elemental beings, human awareness, ancestral and advisory spirits into the world of transpersonal, angelic, spiritual beings. But we do not leave the apparently lower worlds behind, for they are carried with us into their own true higher state; they move through a turning, phase or octave shift also. (The expansions, which are detailed invocations of telesmatic Images, are made at this point.)

This shift is marked by three gong resonances: and the major invocation of the Son of Light begins.

Attributions of Telesmatic Images

The attributes for the invocations to each Quarter (ritual expansion: Cernunnos/Belenos/Briggidda/Arianrhod) are in keeping with those known to us from various sources of Celtic and classical tradition, but they are not limited to academic source material alone. To be effective, any telesmatic image, god-form or goddess-form has to be shaped into the purpose or ceremony for which it is employed. The ancient deities had many varying attributes, and this variety has caused endless and unnecessary confusion to literal-minded pedantic scholars and students. It is not possible in a book of this sort to list and argue the validity of attributes of historical pagan deities, but one of the keys to such attributes is that they change according to the seasons, phases or life-cycle of the image concerned. In magical arts, as in mythology, these transformations may often be shown upon maps such as the Fourfold Circle or the Tree of Life.

A second more technical reason for variations in attributes of deities is that such attributes may – and frequently do – change for specific worship, ritual, visualisation or educational purposes. Thus an image of a goddess, for example, preserved upon a particular temple site, may be carrying an object found nowhere else in connection with such a deity: this merely means that at that location, she had a special function or quality. In magical terms such variations are either purpose-built or divined from the relationship of the telesmatic image to environmental factors (such as springs, forests, hills, caves, or more subtle locii of power within any land or region).

Similarly we find conflicting descriptions of pagan deities in early literature, though there is never any strong disagreement concerning overall attributes and roles. Unusual descriptions are often those relating to functional telesmatic images, perhaps drawn from a ritual, or from a local or specific seasonal traditional teaching. In other words, the gods and goddesses are *not* hard and fast, they are living, transforming entities that relate to one another, and which may from time to time or place to place take on special attributes for particular functions.

Assembling Invocations

When assembling invocations, the magician firstly employs the broad and well-defined attributes of the god-forms or goddess-forms which are to be employed; this method is well-known and there are ample sets of correspondences available for the student to choose from. In our ritual expansion, the Four Images invoked correspond to the primal attributes of the Four Quarters (usually defined by archangels in standard magical arts with a Judaeo-Christian influence). But they also have very specific attributes and powers in their own right: the interaction between these specific attributes and the fundamental powers of the Quarters is vitally important to effective magic. The same Images may be employed at different Quarters, seasons, or phases of the life-cycle, though certain god-forms and goddess-forms are obviously more effective in certain Quarters that relate strongly to their specific roles and attributes. In some cases, the movement of the Image around the Wheel or across it causes the specific functions to alter.

A typical example of this is the form that we have used for the West, Briggidda, Brigit or Bride, in Celtic tradition. She is said in apocryphal tradition to be the foster-mother of Jesus; she has many attributes of light and harmony both as a pagan goddess to whom eternal lights were kept burning, and as a later

Christian saint. She is credited with the provision of nourishment to many people through her totem beast the dun cow (a motif connected to the great Abbeys of Durham and Glastonbury, both of which were built upon major pre-Christian worship sites). These broadly Celtic attributes are often merged with those of a war goddess, known to the Romans as Minerva (from Etruscan origins).

Unlike the more savage fundamental figure of the Morrigan, the great Irish mother goddess of love, sex and death in battle, Briggidda or Brigit has many of the sisterly or even virgin qualities of the classical goddesses Athena and Minerva. The original Celtic goddess, therefore, was a culture goddess who fostered and nourished development, spiritual growth and enlightenment, and acted as a protecting national or tribal power, even to the extent of battle when required. The Roman Minerva fulfilled so many of these requirements that she was taken up easily by those Celts conquered in southern Britain and Europe by the Romans. The name Minerva was preserved by the early chroniclers and historians when describing Celtic goddesses from tradition who had similar attributes to the classical goddess, but were not necessarily identical or true representations of the Roman deity throughout.

In our specific invocation Briggidda is located in the West, where she emphasises her power as benefactor modulated by the Element of Water and the spiritual foundation of Love. If, however, we place her in the East, where her image is modulated by the Element of Air, she appears in her maiden warrior aspect, similar to Minerva or Athena. We then find the warrior-sister, similar to the tarot image of the Chariot,[3] or even to the exaggerated but still valid image of *Britannia*, a revivalist tutelary deity of Britain found on coins, maps and other tokens.

It would be possible to transpose each of our four telesmatic images from Celtic tradition to their opposite Quarter, but we run the risk of weakening the power of the overall ceremony if we do this merely as an intellectual exercise or game of fashionable 'role reversal'. The Guardian, for example,[3] based upon the Celtic Cernunnos or the classical Pan, both being Images of the great keeper of Nature and all life-forces and forms, could be placed in the West. Here his power to tend and protect would be amplified, due to the fundamental attribute of Love as the spiritual consciousness of the Quarter. But by doing so we would modify or under-use many of his most important transformative energies: those very energies which are highly amplified and active when placed in the East as described in our invocation.

What usually occurs in the cyclical movement of Images is a more subtle and vastly more effective process than merely rotating deities around in a superficial manner. If we move one key figure to a suitable and powerful relocation, we find that the other Quarters will generate or attune to Images from the myth cycle or Mystery, but that these Images are not necessarily the original three main deities or telesmatic forms. If we follow our example of Briggidda/Minerva, and move her from the West to the East, she becomes a virgin warrior, an inspirer of thought, cultural development, and a patroness of heroes (rather than a foster mother of spiritual enlightenment). The matrix that we create is not so much one of merely transposing Images, but one of polarity changes within the myth or legend cycle. If we therefore made our male images in each Quarter into female images, and vice-versa, we might use the following four with great effect:

1. East Briggidda/Minerva   Warrior Maiden
2. South Epona   Great Goddess (Horse
                             Goddess)
3. West Mabon   The Divine Youth
4. North Merlin   The Wise Old One

If suitable invocations are constructed to these Images, the overall ceremony will have quite different interim results and imaginative transformations, but will be equally effective in its main function, the Presence of the Son of Light. Such details in the expansion of a ceremony will be important if the central invocation is to be employed for a specific purpose. In our main text, for example, the invocations are designed to bring a maximum energy to bear within the circle, making this energy available for the central ceremony of the Son of Light.

The second pattern described above as one of many possible alternatives would tend towards more particular ends: these are numerous, but we might cite magical education or collective growth towards maturity through challenge and learning as being typical potentials defined by the second pattern. The main invocation would be directed to the West, in our second example, rather than to the East; the presence of the Son of Light then arises through the previously established Image of *Mabon*, the Divine Child, and transforms it into a new reality or state.

Commentary upon the Ritual Expansions

East. The Image employed in the Eastern Quarter is a major god-form within the Western Mysteries. Tradition knows him variously as Cernunnos (from Romano-Celtic inscription) Gwyn ap Nudd (from legend) Herne the Hunter (from folklore); his memory is preserved in a number of British villages with the root word *Cern* in their names (e.g. Cerne Abbas, Cerney). He is Master of the Wild Hunt, Lord of the Animals, and the Guardian of all life, life-forms, and transformative energies. Variants of this force exist in traditions worldwide. In the context of transformative energies, the telesmatic Image of the Guardian transcends the primal function of herdsman and hunter, though it is often expressed through such functions.

In his transcendent role he acts both as a focus and as a mediating entity for higher energies and consciousness connected to catabolic universal forces. The Guardian is known as the great Initiator, for without his purifying influence, we may not progress towards enlightenment. As a deity this form has had a popular revival in modern paganism, though frequently limited to the animal generative aspect of his power, which is only one of the lesser manifestations. In classical mythology he is known as Pan the god of nature, and the originator of the word *panic*. There is no doubt that this figure brings that 'fear of the Lord that inspires wisdom'. In folklore and legend he is a terrifying all-powerful entity, and this holds good for invocation in magical arts.

This is not a god-form for cosy spiritualised therapeutic meanderings: his major power is to look within each and every creature and perceive whatever is corrupt or imbalanced therein. No wonder his presence is terrifying, for he offers us the choice between facing up to our own weaknesses and evils and accepting his purifying energies, or turning back upon ourselves and remaining stagnant in full awareness of our stagnation. This last state is the 'sin against the holy spirit': perceiving truth but refusing to accept it or act upon it.

The Guardian is visualised and mediated by the officer of the East, and other celebrants may contribute to the image-building. Each officer of a Quarter, however, should concentrate primarily upon invoking his or her god-form, and then mediating that form and holding it steady for the central invocation of the Son of Light. There is a simple but by no means inflexible order of priorities for rituals of this sort, which shows how officers may employ their energies:

1st priority: invocation and mediation of allotted power or Image.

2nd priority: invocation and mediation of polar opposite/partner image (East to West, North to South, and so forth).

3rd priority: awareness and response to Images on right and left hand (generally in Quarters, but sometimes as specific forms built upon the Cross-Quarters of North-East, South-East, South-West, North-West). (See Figure 17.)

The First Priority

When the ceremony leads towards a central Image, as in the Ritual of the Son of Light, the officers of the Quarters may operate in a number of different ways. The general training is to maintain the force or image of each Quarter, mediating it and holding it in balance with the other Images around the Circle. In this instance the Mediator, who is the priest or priestess of the Centre, is left to work upon the major invocation of the Light, and the more subtle transformative operations are left to the non-human entities such as the Images, innerworld contacts, ancestral spirits, and the angelic and elemental entities present within the assembled convocation. This is all standard practice and highly effective.

An alternative method is for the officers of the Quarters to step out of their Images, so to speak, and join in the central invocation of the Presence by pouring their energies towards the central mediator. This is a more subtle technique, and should be defined beforehand by discussion and intent. Operating in this manner is often impressive: the officer for each Quarter stands before the god-form or goddess-form, which is slightly behind them and within the opened Gate of the respective Quarter. The telesmatic Image acts as a lens for energy, projecting it into the human, who in turn projects it towards the central Mediator (not necessarily into image-building, for reasons which are described below). The central mediator receives the full power of the Circle, and transforms it into the invocation of the Son of Light. (See Figure 18.)

This bridging, mediating or *lens* effect is further heightened by the presence of other entities or imaginal forms beyond the opened gates: they support the major telesmatic Images, or in some circumstance enter through the gates and are positioned at the cross-Quarters.

The Second Priority

The invocation of the polar opposite or partner image is of great value in advanced magical arts, but must be handled with a certain amount of caution. For the present purpose we will assume that readers are aware of some of the basic typical problems of magical practice, such as the transference of emotional charge to a human officer within or after a ritual, rather than to the core of the ceremony itself. The second priority is carried out after a powerful god- or goddess-form or other entity is fully attuned to the ritualist's imagination and vital energies; he or she is in an altered and empowered state of consciousness. The visualisation and polar-mediation of the partner Image (usually in the opposite Quarter) is therefore full of magical implications.

Perhaps the simplest option would seem to be that such partners are actual partners in their regular outer life: lovers, husband and wife if the Images have sexual relationship, or brothers or sisters (in function or life-style if not in flesh and blood) if the Images are harmonic or non-sexually defined. This often works, but it can be the source of potential disruption of outer life just as easily as the more commonly known emotional transference to magical lovers. The secret is always in the trained ability to mediate the Images and then disengage properly.

When mediating the polar opposite, an officer or ritualist may either (a) step out of the Image slightly, and *as a human* counter-mediate the polar opposite Image (i.e. Male to Female, North to South and so forth) or (b) conduct the polar mediation in the role of his or her primary Image. This second method is the most potent, and therefore the most potentially difficult. For

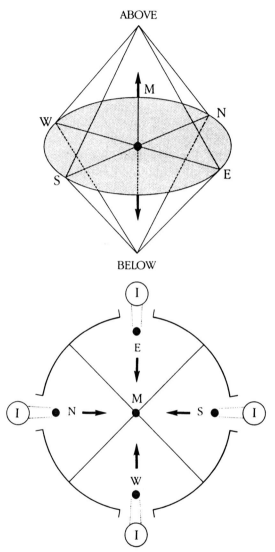

Figure 18   Power Patterns in Mediation

I: Innerworld Power or Telesmatic Image

example, the officer of the **South** in our present ritual takes the Image of *Belenos, Lord of the Assembly of the Sun*, upon himself: when the officer of the **North** invokes Arianrhod, **South** also invokes and counter-mediates the goddess, as if he is Belenos calling to Ariadne. If this procedure is followed throughout the circle (assuming the officers are capable of mediation and visualisation of such a complex nature) the energy is amplified to a very high degree.

The Third Priority

Awareness of the Images employed to the right and left of the officer is more valuable than it might seem at first glance. In general practice everyone gets on with their own task in a ceremony, and the fusion of forces is organic and harmonic. It must be stressed here that over-concentration on peripherals at the expense of a central or major Image is a sure way to destroy any collective force assembled: but providing we realise that it is a *third* priority, we may consider the relationship between the officer of a Quarter and that Quarter's Pillars or Cross Quarters. We may also consider the relationship generated between the officer and the main Quarters to his or her right and left hand.

The essence of this polarised awareness is similar to the genuine tradition of pathworking (as opposed to the general visualising which is often incorrectly called 'pathworking' in modern magical or meditational literature). While the officer of each Quarter does not concentrate specifically upon those Images or forces to his or her right and left hand, a general response to and awareness of these forces cause a pressure or fusion of energies which will support each person in his or her individual role. This can be easily seen in the standard diagram of a squared circle, for which we can assume not only that the Quarters reflect power *across* the centre to each other, but that each Quarter projects force to the right and left (see Figure 19).

When we have officers with supporters or sub-officers on either side of them we generate the complex energy patterns shown in Figure 20. This increasing complexity is then reduced by mutual definition to a specific working pattern (such as a triangle, serpentine or 'Z' sign) while the full polarity grid or glyph resonates as an undertone or framework. Traditionally the Elementals maintain this framework in a ritual.

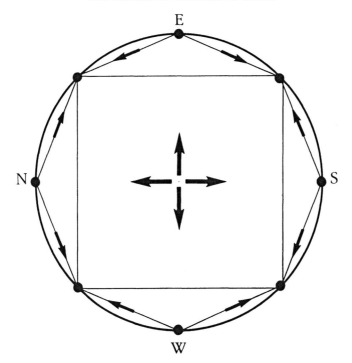

Figure 19   The Cross-Quarters and Energy Flow

Invocation of the South

Several magical and metaphysical traditions are found within
this invocation, but they are all harmonically related and fused
within the overall Image of Bel or Belenos. This deity was the
solar or light god of the British and European Celts, similar in
many ways to the Irish god Lugh, but possibly an older form.

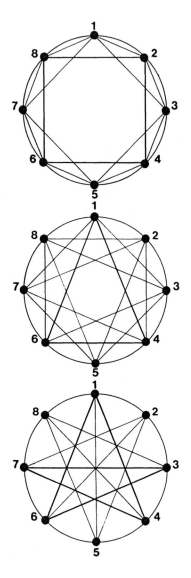

Figure 20   Polarity Patterns

He is visualised in the present context as an adult male figure riding upon a white mare. The Mare connects to the other telesmatic form viable for a Celtic ceremony, the goddess Epona. It should be stressed that the concept of a 'pure' image is nonsense when using telesmata, though it might apply in geometrics or use of Platonic solids in visualisation. The god- and goddess-forms have harmonic entities or variations inherent within them: otherwise they become stereotypes or sterile shapes that cannot work. Thus Belenos, the god-form of the ascended sun in midsummer, rides upon the mare, which is the totem beast of the Great Goddess. His power is intimately related to that of his female counterpart, be she sister or lover.

In the invocation, however, Bel or Belenos is located upon the South, his major position of full power: the feminine counterpart, therefore, is implicit rather than explicit, for the Goddess is explicitly stated in the West and North, where a male Image would be implicit.

The Image of Belenos is one of victorious light, a perfectly balanced noonday and midsummer of energy and consciousness. He often appears masked, just as goddess images are frequently found veiled. The light of his face may be too strong to look upon directly, for he does not have a human component, unlike the Son of Light who may appear in human form but with full power. Incarnations of Bel or Lugh or similar powers tend to be heroes with specific tasks, rather than saviours or redeemers. Belenos corresponds in many ways to the Greek Apollo, though he is found bearing a lance or spear rather than a bow.

The spear is the upright balance or rod, implement of the Element of Fire; it also represents the Middle Pillar of the Tree of Life, or the upper part of the Spindle of the Worlds, reaching from Sun to Stars. The tarot trumps associated with this area of metaphysics and consciousness are of course The Sun and The Star. Each telesmatic image contains within itself indicators of further or balancing qualities and energies: thus Belenos points his spear towards the stars, to the North where his polar partner the goddess Arianrhod rules.

Belenos (closely related both in cultural history, religion and metaphysics to the Archangel Michael used in magical arts based upon Judaeo-Christian symbolism) is seen to lead or open the way for a host of innerworld beings. This is one of the most important inner aspects of the ceremony, for many powerful forces are focused upon the central intent of the ritualists through this operation. Initially the vision refers to the ancient tradition that ancestral souls are united together, and that their light becomes the sun.

More specifically it refers to a collective consciousness which both draws upon and originates specific individuals who operate the Mysteries of Light. In very early cultures these were sacred kings and queens, Priests and Priestesses. Such forms remain active within the deeper levels of awareness, accessible through meditation and visualisation. On rare occasions it is possible for an individual (not a group *en masse*) to become a member of this harmonic structure or Mystery while still expressing a physical body. Tradition teaches that certain effective priests, priestesses and men and women of spiritual potency have incarnated intentionally from this Mystery or Convocation. In such a case, the initiation would be a process of remembering rather than joining for the first time.

The Perpetual Assembly sits in the City of Light. This city is another major concept within the Mysteries, and may be experienced to great effect in individual or group visualisation. The City is one of the resonant dwelling places of the Grail, and holds many subsidiary mysteries, potencies and gatherings. Like all magical realities, it is both a state of consciousness (in this case a specific attuned collective consciousness of solar qualities) and an actual place or dimension. The experienced magician eventually ceases to waste time over the distinctions between states and places, for even modern materialist science now affirms that they are interchangeable.

Progress around the Circle

Just as the Wheel of Life or Circle progresses through a Fourfold cycle or spiral, so do the specific Images invoked in any ritual. It would be pointless and unproductive to use telesmatic forms that did not relate to one another; this relationship is one of the most valuable contents of any tradition or school of magic and mythology. With the first invocation of Cernunnos, the Guardian, a wild and in many ways uncontrollable and unpredictable power was aroused within the Circle. Each officer undertook to meet and relate to this power come what may, for the Guardian brings all secrets to the surface, and transforms the bodies and souls of humanity even beyond physical death.

With the second invocation, of Bel, an equally potent force is given an ancient and effective form. This power brings illumination, a zenith of vital energies, and a balance and victory over opposing factors that might lead to collapse of the ritual. The Image of Belenos harmonises the wild energies of Cernunnos, but it must be stated that without the power of the East, that of the South might not arise at all. This simple truth is often forgotten in magical arts; we cannot necessarily or arbitrarily summon a power or form without the preceding and relative powers and forms. Attempts to raise entities in a single or unharmonic event can lead to inverse states, problems or, more usually, failure. While it is possible, and advisable, to meditate upon and visualise each Image separately before uniting them, such isolation of Images is for training and higher contemplation, not for effective ritual. Thus each of the Four Powers in the Circle is independent of, yet inseparably related to, each of the others. The initial cycle of relationship is of course sunwise around the Circle from East to North. We may now return to our commentary upon the invocations for each Quarter.

Invocation of the West

The major Image of Brigid, Briggidda or Bride incorporates a number of other images. It must be emphasised that in a different context, these images may become major telesmata; this organic and holographic property of magical images is vital to success in visualisation and ritual. Many students, and regrettably some experienced magicians, tend to find the fusion and separation of images a problem. Authors of books on esoteric or mythical and magical symbolism frequently receive irate letters from rigid persons who are upset because the sole interpretation with which they can cope, of perhaps a tarot card or divine image, has been varied or challenged. The working magician, however, should be able to attune to a specific image for a specific ceremony, and then re-attune to a variant form in a different context. Magic is not, after all, a dogmatic religion.

The feminine Image for the West, employed in our ritual text, has the following attributes:

1. *Perfect Love*: She is a feminine archetype giving form to the spiritual force of Love.

2. *Purification*: She purifies, through the power of Love, the processes of creation and manifestation. Thus her power is not confined or stereotyped into an emotional or kindly oversimplification; she has an aspect of catabolic or destroying power, without which no purification may be achieved. The Officer for the West should visualise the rhythm of tides in connection with this Image, for she gives and withdraws equally. There is a further reference here to the tides of the Lunar World, and the Mysteries of Birth which are placed in the West in magical arts. The orthodox Christian and mystical Kabbalistic connection is the Archangel Gabriel and the Annunciation, but this is merely one aspect of an enduring Mystery of special conception and birth, long established and practised in the ancient religions and within specific schools or innerworld orders.

3. During the visualisation of this figure, robed in blue-green and silver, with a radiant star upon her brow, She incorporates *attributes of Venus*. But it must be clear to the officer of the West that this Image is not solely Venus; if the power is modified to work through the image of Venus alone, many important connectives and potentials are lost.

4. *Her totem beast is the Dun Cow*. This is seen as a white cow, carrying upon her back a copper cauldron with a crystal rim. The cow is the beast of fertility and nourishment, and in British legends the Dun Cow is said to have fed multitudes through her perpetual milk pouring into a cauldron or bucket. Here we have a prototype of the Grail, connected to a totem animal that is, in fact, one form of the Great Goddess. We may see it as an agricultural motif or from the tribal nomadic cattle rearing culture of the ancient Celts; but it has, like many such legends, a stellar analogy. The flood of milk from the divine Cow is the Milky Way, the river of stars. This concept is found in the central Invocation of the Son of Light, in the words 'his the rainbow letters all in rich fermented milk'.

5. The Lady is guardian of the Blessed Isles, the paradisal primal lands to the uttermost west. Thus she incorporates the image of *Morgen*, the priestess of the mysteries of regeneration and healing, a druidic figure found in early legends such as the *Vita Merlini*.[3]

The Invocation of the North

The Image for the North is called Arianrhod (from rota, a Wheel), the Lady of the Silver Wheel. She is visualised as a dark and uncompromising figure; there is nothing kindly, gentle or human about her. She is an image that embodies, in anthropomorphic form, the truth of relative states: her power is that terrifying understanding that we touch when we compare our lives to those of stars.

Her attributes are:

1. *A Silver Wheel*: sometimes identified with specific constellations, or more generally the geocentric image of stars circling in the night sky. This motif also applies to the Wheel of Judgement, of the great cycle of stellar consciousness. In a human sense it refers to our cycle of birth, death and rebirth.

2. *She is crowned with silver and crystal*: silver is the Lunar metal, denoting the light of the Eye of Night. In a broader sense it is also the colour associated with stars. Crystal upon the crown reveals that the Mysteries of the deepest mineral world are exalted by the Goddess of the Stars; the UnderWorld is equally her realm. While we saw a crystal rim upon a copper cauldron in the West, which denoted that Mysteries of regeneration were composed of earth and water, we find the crystal now upon the Crown, showing that the ultimate poles of universal Being, spirit and matter, stars and stones, are at one in the Goddess.

3. *Her totem animals are the Bear, Owl and Wren.*
(a) Bear: symbolises great strength and endurance, protection of young, and by association the Mystery of the Bee, or the collective power of the Earth as an organic entity made of many separate parts. Many historical goddesses of the ancient world were associated with bears, bees, honey and the emblem of the hive. There is further stellar connection to the Great Bear, and to the wide spectrum of totemism associated with King Arthur. The bear survived as a totem of stewardship (to the rightful king) in Britain as late as the eighteenth century.[2]
(b) The Owl is the UnderWorld bird, associated with the grim chthonic goddess Hecate in classical myth. It is also the bird of Athena, or wisdom, and is associated with feminine personae in Celtic legend.
(c) The Wren is the bird of the Sacrificing Goddess and her beloved victim, the Sacred King, the smallest creature that is also the greatest.

The Centre

Having worked our way in some detail through the ceremony, its symbolism, background, expansions and its various alternative arrangements of image, no detailed commentary needs to be given for the central invocation. The culminating and concluding operations of the ceremony, as described in the ritual script, are self-explanatory.

11

THE INCANTATION: A CREATION RITUAL

1: In the beginning the Spirit of All-Being
Becomes breath within the Void,
And utters forth Four Sounds of Power
Through Seven Gates of One Creation.
Each Sound proclaims a Name re-echoing
Its Origin in Spirit. [*Here Four Vowels and Calls are resonated.*]
In each Name breath of One Being lives
Yet each itself becomes a being,
Four in One
United by One Sound.

Know that at the height and depth
Of Seven levels of Creation
Two faces of one truth are found –
One the Father of the Stars
One the Mother of the Deep,
United and conjoined for ever
In the Living Child of Light. [*Arms raised in invocation.*]

2: In the Name of the Star Father
The Child of Light passes to and fro
Within without the utter Void.
He speaks His Word between Two Dragons –
One reaching to extremity of night and depth,
One reaching to extremity of day and height.
One is coiling time and space
One is coiling power and stars;
Weaving together they enfold the Void
Which draws the heart of Being In and Out.

Through their enfoldment of the Void
The Bright One passes to and fro
According to his will:

As a breath of Air
As a tongue of Fire
As a drop of Water
As a Crystal, clear and perfect. [*Here a crystal is uplifted and placed upon the altar.*]

3: It is in His Name
That peace is now declared,
It is in His Name that power is now declared:
I am a Light and a Keeper of Lights
I am a Mask of the Bright One
I bring Light unto the Darkness
And Darkness to the Light.
In me are all guardians, kings and priests
Partaking of the Mystery of Weaving;
The Keys and Keystones are my Knowledge
The Stars and Starstones are my Wisdom
The Bright One is my Understanding
On the Hanging Tree
Reversed through space and time. [*Stands in posture of Hanged Man (i.e. right foot behind left knee, arms upraised). Pause/meditate remaining in posture.*]

4: In the Name of the Great Mother [*Stands on both feet.*]
I speak now as Guardian of the Threshold
Where Light and Dark weave together;
My Right Hand is a black devouring serpent [*Lowers right hand.*]
My Left Hand is a bright flaming serpent [*Lowers left hand.*]
My heart is a wheel of crystal fire
My feet transform the secret waiting earth
My brow reveals the Eye of Light, all-seeing. [*Touches both hands to brow.*]

Behold the Mystery of the Star Father
Behold the Mystery of the Deep Mother
Behold their Being One in Light. [*Flame light reflects through crystal.*]

5: Water falls upon the earth [*Water sprinkled on crystal.*]
And seed becomes growing grain;
Corn becomes bread
Bread becomes body

Body becomes crystal
Through the power of the secret Fire [*Hands laid upon crystal.*]

Water becomes wine
Wine becomes blood
Blood becomes starlight
Starlight becomes spirit
Spirit becomes crystal
Through the power of the secret earth. [*Hands crossed over crystal (left over right).*]

This is the body of spirit
In a most perfect form –
The breath of life is upon it
The star fire of light lives within it,
Like unto like across the Void.
Breath and Light
Blood and body
Stars in Worlds
Bright One in Earth. [*Contemplation of crystal.*]

His the Right Hand
His the Left Hand
His the Rainbow Letters
Spiralled in most perfect dragon form:
Not Seven but Four
Not Four but Two
Not Two but One
In One Being unity
Unbeing . . . AMEN [*Close of ceremony.*]

12

THE MERLIN RITUAL

This short text is the basis for a ritual that may be extended in operation; within the basic script there are several areas where action, contemplation and visualisation replace mere words. The setting is *The Mystery of Merlin* as found in the *Prophecies and Life of Merlin*, and to a lesser extent in the Welsh legends of the *Mabinogion*. These are essential reading for anyone wishing to enter the Mystery; they are magical, legendary and prophetic texts of Celtic tradition, but have many parallels and connective traditions worldwide.[3]

The central Image and Power for invocation is feminine, named as the Daughter or Child of Light. She is visualised as a young woman veiled in light, and has many of the attributes attached to the goddess Brigit, who later became St Bride. But she has more than a Western European or Celtic ambience: she is the feminine solar power, and the feminine Saviour or Redeemer. Although this power is generally defined as male, invoking it in female form results in a remarkable and powerful response. The spiritual power itself is, of course, androgynous, being beyond polar definition but our imaginative forms are vitally important in practical magic, as they are the vehicles for forces that could not otherwise be made active or accessible to consciousness.

The Creation of the Worlds

Personae
Taliesin (East), Instructor in the Mystery Tradition: Priest.
Bladud (South), Sacred King: Hero.

Morgen (West), Regeneratrix: Priestess.
Ariadne (North), Queen: Goddess.

Functions of each Officer
East: Summons the Wind and powers of Purification.
South: Summons Fire and the Company of Blessed Ancestors in Light.
West: Summons Water and the powers of Regeneration.
North: Summons Earth/Stars and the powers of Transformation.

(Purification, Illumination, Regeneration, Transformation)

Personae (2)
Guendoloena (South-East), Mediates power of Spring.
Rhodarch (South-West), Mediates power of Summer.
Ganieda (North-West), Mediates power of Autumn.
Merlin (North-East), Mediates power of Winter and transition from Inner world: *No representing Officer.*
The Company: Men are the company of Chieftains; women are the company of Seeresses.
Herald: Questions or challenges/invites as indicated below.

[*The central light is lit by the Officer of the South.*]

1. *Opening reading from* Vita Merlini: *The Creation*[2]
   Meanwhile Taliesin had come to see Merlin the prophet who had sent for him to find out what wind or rainstorm was coming up, for both together were drawing near and the clouds were thickening. He drew the following illustrations under the guidance of Minerva his associate.
   'Out of nothing the Creator of the world produced four [elements] that they might be the prior cause as well as the material for creating all things when they were joined together in harmony: the heaven which He adorned with stars and which stands on high and embraces everything like the shell surrounding a nut; then He made the air, fit for forming sounds, through the medium of which day and night present the stars; the sea which girds the land in four circles, and with its mighty refluence so strikes the air as to generate the winds which are said to be four in number; as a foundation He placed the earth, standing by its own strength and not lightly moved, which is divided into five parts, whereof the middle one is not habitable

because of the heat and the two furthest are shunned because of their cold. To the last two He gave a moderate temperature and these are inhabited by men and birds and herds of wild beasts. He added clouds to the sky so that they might furnish sudden showers to make the fruits of the trees and of the ground grow with their gentle sprinkling. With the help of the sun these are filled like water skins from the rivers by a hidden law, and then, rising through the upper air, they pour out the water they have taken up, driven by the force of the winds. From them come rainstorms, snow, and round hail when the cold damp wind breathes out its blasts which, penetrating the clouds, drive out the streams just as they make them. Each of the winds takes to itself a nature of its own from its proximity to the zone where it is born. Beyond the firmament in which He fixed the shining stars He placed the ethereal heaven and gave it as a habitation to troops of angels whom the worthy contemplation and marvellous sweetness of God refresh throughout the ages. This also He adorned with stars and the shining sun, laying down the law, by which the star should run within fixed limits through the part of heaven entrusted to it. He afterwards placed beneath this the airy heavens, shining with the lunar body, which throughout their high places abound in troops of spirits who sympathise or rejoice with us as things go well or ill. They are accustomed to carry the prayers of men through the air and to beseech God to have mercy on them, and to bring back intimations of God's will, either in dreams or by voice or by other signs, through doing which they become wise. The space below the moon abounds in daemons, who are skilled in the matter of dreams; often they assume a body made of air and appear to us and many things often follow. They even hold intercourse with women and make them pregnant, generating in a mysterious manner. So therefore He made the heavens to be inhabited by three orders of spirits that each one might look out for something and renew the world from the renewed seed of things.

2. **Herald:** Are there Four within this space to speak for the Four Powers?

3. The Four Main Officers declare as follows:

East: I am named Taliesin; It was I who taught the patterns of Creation of the Universe to the questing Merlin, according to the ancient and enduring tradition of the Mysteries of Life.

South: I am named Bladud; it was I who opened the Gates to the Otherworld, when they were sought by the magician Merlin according to the Mysteries of Light.

West: I am named Morgen; it was I who took the travelling sage Merlin in to the Fortunate Isle of the West for his regeneration through the Mysteries of Love.

North: I am named Ariadne; it was I who gave the vision of eternity to the prophet Merlin when his perceptions flew up to the stars through the Mysteries of Universal Law.

4. **Herald:** How shall these Mysteries be made One today to recreate the World?

5. **East:** By the power vested in me I invoke the Element of Air that all corruption shall be purified and made clean. [*Invokes.*]

South: By the power vested in me I invoke the Element of Fire and the Company of Illuminated and Blessed Kings and Heroes, that all seeds of new beginnings shall flourish and grow strong, by the fire of innermost power made manifest in the outer world. [*Invokes.*]

West: By the power vested in me I invoke the Element of Water that nourishes and distills regeneration and rebirth [*Invokes.*]

North: By the power vested in me I invoke the perfect Element of Earth, that the wonder of the stars may be reflected within the regenerated world now and for ever.

6. **Herald:** How shall these great powers be made manifest?

Ganieda: Through the fullness of the questing, fruitful mind may a perfect kingdom be enabled.

Guendoloena: Through the rising, growing joy of balanced feelings shall that same perfect kingdom be enlivened.

Rodarch: Through honourable and immaculate deeds and works shall that perfect kingdom be made whole.

Herald: In the North-East stands a misty figure, waiting at the point of spiralling, the place of transition; no one person here may speak for him, for he is Merlin in the past, in the present, and in the future. His role is to fuse these powers as one, to make ready for the Blessed Son of Light within the centre of our circle of creation.

7. **East:**   Who stands for the ultimate roots of the World?

The Company: We all stand, then, now and for ever.

East: Who stands for the Plants of the World?

Company: We all stand, then, now and for ever.

East: Who stands for the creatures of the World?

Company: We all stand, then, now and for ever.

East: Who stands for the Men and Women of the World?

Company: We all stand, then, now and for ever.

8. **South:**   Who will stand for the Earth?
Who will stand for the Moon?
Who will stand for the Sun?
Who will stand for the Stars?
Who will stand for the great primal Dragons?
Who will stand for the First and Last Breath of Being?

North: In the pattern of the Weaving moved the Daughter of Light: She who spoke through Merlin, who hung upon the Tree of Triple Death, her hair spreading through the burning river of time, her hands extended in blessing and compassion upon all who suffer, all who live in ignorance and darkness.

West: By the secret way across the Abyss of the Great Waters she comes, tempering all powers into one harmonious choir; she passes to and fro between the worlds and the void according to her will and waits, now, only for our willing recognition . . .

South: Let us pause now, and willingly recognise the Child of Light that has come among us. [*Invokes as required.*]

[*Pause for contemplation*]

9. **South:**   Blessed is the Daughter of Light that comes among us
Blessed is the Light that lives within us,
Blessed is our Being One in Light.
In the Name of the Star Father,

The Earth Mother,
The True Taker
And the Great Giver. [*Intones* AMEN]

Now is the time of transition, carried by the figure of Merlin standing in the North-East: he bids us take a new image of the world and send it forth according to the hallowed methods of our Mystery.

East: Through this Eastern Gate the World is renewed . . .

West: Through this Western Gate the World is renewed . . .

North: Through this Northern Gate the World is renewed . . .

South: Through this Southern Gate the World is renewed . . .

Herald: Three Wheels are known in our Mysteries, the Wheel of Fortune, the Wheel of Adjustment, and the Wheel of the Universal Judgement . . . let the members of this Company pass forth into a new world, each according to the Wheel that he or she understands.

East: Let there be peace between us and the East.

South: Let there be peace between us and the South.

West: Let there be peace between us and the West.

North: Let there be peace between us and the North.

All Officers: In the heights and in the depths let there be peace now and for ever.

[**Herald** leaves hall, leaving door open for others to follow. **South** extinguishes central light when required.]

13

THE WEAVING
RITUAL

May be conducted by any number of people by allocating roles around the Circle as defined in the script.

Officers
East: Mediates the **Ace of Swords** and the **Mother of the Whirlwind.** May adopt the personae of *(a) King/Queen of Swords* or *(b) in Judaeo-Christian imagery the Archangel Raphael.*

South: Mediates the **Ace of Rods** and the **Mother of the Blazing Light.** May adopt the personae of *King/Queen of Rods* or *the Archangel Michael.*

West: Mediates the **Ace of Cups** and the *Mother of the Boundless Ocean.* May adopt the personae of *King/Queen of Cups* or *the Archangel Gabriel.*

North: Mediates the **Ace of Shields** and the *Mother of Eternal Night.* May adopt the personae of *King/Queen of Shields* or *the Archangel Uriel.*

North-East and Centre: *The Opener of Gates.*

[Further officers are aligned according to each Quarter: the North-East may have two supporting officers on his/her right or left.]

1. *The ceremony begins in total darkness and silence. All present turn attention inwards towards Peace. (The* **Opener** *is able to light the* first candle by touch alone, from practice.)

2. **Opener:** Peace is a secret unknown.

All: Still are the voices that echoed alone.

Opener: Open the gates of the starways. [*Lights flame in centre.*]

All: Gone are the places of whispering stones.

Opener utters Elemental Calls *E I O A U.*

All utter Elemental Calls and chant AMEN.

3. **Opener:** From one thread of light are all words woven
And no single part is severed from the whole.
Let us summon the power of the Weaver here
among us
According to the pattern of the mystery.

[*Takes taper and lights it from central flame; passes to* **East.**]

4. **East:** [*Lights Eastern flame.*]
I call upon the power of the East
To awaken and attend through this blessed gate.

[*Utters Elemental Call of Air.*]

By the power of the Kings of Air
By the power of the Sword of Dawn
In the name of the Mother of the Whirlwind.

[*Hands taper to* **South.**]

5. **South:** I call upon the power of the South
To arise and attend through this Blessed Gate.

[*Utters Elemental Call of Fire.*]

By the power of the Kings of Fire
By the power of the Rod of Bright Noonday
In the name of the Mother of Blazing Fire.

[*Hands taper to* **West.**]

6. **West:** I call upon the power of the West.
To increase and attend through this Blessed Gate.

[*Utters Elemental Call of Water.*]

By the power of the Kings of Water
By the power of the Cup of Sunset
In the name of the Mother of the Boundless Ocean

[*Hands taper to* **North.**]

7. **North:** I call upon the power of the North
To appear and attend through this Blessed Gate.

[*Utters Elemental Call of Earth.*]

In the name of the Kings of Earth
By the power of the Mirror of Stars
In the name of the Mother of Eternal Night

8. [**All** *reiterate Elemental Calls around the Circle and resonate* AMEN,
then turn to focus attention upon the central light.]

9. **East:** Now for you I weave some weaving
Listen to it well,
Now for you I twist some twining
Listen to its spell:

10. **All:** (a) Once I was held in the Eyes of the Night
(b) Once in the Voice of the Day
(c) Once in the arms of a Child Alone
(d) And once in the Mind of a Stone

[*(a) Arms raised in the sign of Stars; (b) Arms held out level in the sign
of Sun; (c) Arms crossed in the sign of Humanity; (d) Arms held
downwards in the sign of the Earth.*]

11. **East:** In and in the words are weaving
Through these eyes so blind
Through and through you hold my weaving
In your own design.

[*Pause before proceeding.*]

12. **East:** Once I gained a seed from the Dawn.
South: Once the jewel from a nest.
North: Once the light from a fair lady's mirror.
West: Once a word from the West.

13. **West:** Now it is ending slow your breathing
Now your joys are mine
Through and through you hold my weaving
In your own design.

14. **All:** Gone are the places of whispering stones
Open the gates of the starways
Still are the voices that echoed alone
Peace is a secret unknown.

Opener *chants* AMEN: *all chant* AMEN.

15. **Opener:**   Let us now utter the ancient words of power used in this Mystery since the worlds were first reflected and uttered through time and space: by the power vested in me as Opener of the Way I open out the name of the Dark Mother Below.

[*Chants an elongated* AMA.]

16. **Opener:**   By the power vested in me as Opener of the Way I open out the name of the Bright Mother of Light.

[*Chants an elongated* AIMA.]

17. **Opener:**   By the power of the assembled company in all worlds let us utter now the name of Unity and Peace.

[**All** *chant an elongated* AMEN.]

18. *The chant is now reiterated by all present three times as follows.*

AMA AIMA AMEN . . . AMA AIMA AMEN . . . AMA AIMA AMEN.

19. [*A circle dance begins led by* **East** (*if space permits*): *all except* **Opener** *move E/S/W/N arousing the energies of each Quarter as they pass.*]

20. [**Opener** *allows energies to build as required, then strikes a gong three times.* **East** *now changes direction of dance to pass E/S/N/W three times. After third* **Z** *movement, officers return sunwise to their stations.*]

Alternative method in restricted space

19.(a)   [*A chant begins led by* **East** *chanting vowel sounds around the Circle: E I O A/ E I O A/ E I O A; the rotation is sunwise.*]

20.(a)   [**Opener** *allows energies to build, then strikes gong three times.* **East** *now changes direction of the chant by raising the level of pitch by one tone: the chant then travels E/S/N/W using vowel order of E I A O/ E I A O/ E I A O.*]

21.   [*On conclusion of chant or dance (or both)* **Opener** *moves to centre of circle and raises arms in sign of invocation.*]

Opener: As summoned I dance through a second advance
To lessen the learning you turn
But for most of the rhyme I'm a fool out of time
Who grieves you in sorrow to yearn

For when time is a ring and the second a king
To the kin that is locked in the left
In seeking the me of your turning a key
I deft of your body bereft
Am a fire in a light
A star in a night
A side in the stone of a hill
A branch of the leaf
In the path of the thief
And the answer is:
Be what you will.

And if you dare suppose to bethorn who arose
As a dawn at the crest of the Sun
The answering name is forgettably plain
In growing to love:
Be at One.

[*A pause here for silent meditation.*]

22. **North:**   In the name of the Mother of Eternal Night
I declare our Mystery manifest

South: In the name of the Mother of Blazing Fire
I declare our Mystery illuminated

West: In the name of the Mother of the Boundless Ocean
I declare our Mystery fulfilled

East: In the name of the Mother of the Whirlwind
I declare our Mystery dispersed.

Opener: Manifest, illuminate, fulfil, disperse.

All: So is the world seeded with truth.

Opener: Let us now close the gates of the Mystery of the
Weaver, and depart in peace.

[*Each officer closes his or her Gate by sign, extinguishing the lights in
the order of:* **West/South/North/East**.]

23. **Opener** *extinguishes the central light using the Crossing Formula
as follows.*]

In the name of the Star Father
The Earth Mother
The True Taker
The Great Giver
One Being of Light.

[*All resonate* AMEN *and depart in silence.*]

AFTERWORD

The main part of this book has been concerned with practical experience and experiment. Certain areas have been left open intentionally, as the completion is found inwardly; a great deal of magical art is fulfilled through *events*, and these events should lead to transformation and spiritual insight, or what is nowadays broadly termed an altered state of consciousness.

Anyone who works with the visualisations and dramatic ceremonies suggested in our examples is welcome to write (care of the Publisher) to the author. All serious letters or reports or queries will be answered if possible, but the author is not qualified to answer personal problems or matters of religious dispute or conviction.

There are no orders or societies, in the outer world, that represent the Mysteries described in our text: any that claim to do so should be subjected to strict scrutiny, particularly if money is required for membership or other matters supposedly connected to the Mystery. If we work steadily with structures of symbolism and concepts such as those used in the foregoing chapters, there is, and never will be, any need to join groups or societies. Ultimately membership of a Mystery is an organic or harmonic change of awareness; when this occurs many fellow members are contacted and discovered.

APPENDIX

Lullay: or The Corpus Christi Carol

Refrain: *Lullay lullay lullay lullay,*
The falcon hath born my make [mate] away:

The Heron flew east and the Heron flew west,
She flew over a fair forest:
She flew up and she flew down
She flew over an orchard brown
In that orchard there stands a Hall
Covered all over in purple and pall
In that Hall there lyeth a bed
Covered all over with purple and red
On that bed there lyeth a knight
His wounds do bleed with main and might
From his wounds there runneth a flood
The one half water and the other half blood
At the bed's foot there lyeth a hound
That licks off the blood as it daily runs down
A maiden sits beside the bed
Sewing upon a silver thread
At the bed's foot there stands a stone
With Corpus Christi written thereon
By the bed's head there flowers a thorn
That never so blossomed since Adam was born

*(There are other variants of this traditional, originally
medieval carol.)*

BIBLIOGRAPHICAL
NOTES

1. Stewart, R. J., *Living Magical Arts*, Blandford Press, Poole, 1987.
2. Stewart, R. J., *The Prophetic Vision of Merlin; The Mystic Life of Merlin*, both Arkana, London and Boston 1986/7. These analyse the twelfth-century Merlin texts by Geoffrey of Monmouth which are a major source for magical transformative traditions from bardic and classical sources. Also Tolstoy, N., *The Quest for Merlin*, Hamish Hamilton, 1986, for a detailed historical study of Merlin in early sources. Also *The Book of Merlin*, ed. R. J. Stewart, Blandford Press, Poole, 1987, for a collection of insights into Merlin and British legends by various authors. Also *The Second Book of Merlin*: both volumes are the collected papers of The Merlin Conference held annually in London. Thorpe, L., *The History of The Kings of Britain* (trans.) Harmondsworth, 1966. The modern translation of the major work by Geoffrey of Monmouth.
3. Stewart, R. J., *The Merlin Tarot*, A detailed study of the early tarot imagery and cosmology in the *Vita Merlini*, plus a full-colour deck of cards restating the Images for modern use, painted by Miranda Gray, Aquarian Press, Wellingborough, 1988.
4. Stewart, R. J., *The UnderWorld Initiation*, Aquarian Press, Wellingborough, 1985/1989. Also *Where is Saint George? Pagan imagery in English folksong*, Moonraker Press, 1976 (UK); Humanities Press, New Jersey, 1977 (USA). Republished in paperback by Blandford Press, Poole, 1988.
5. Gilbert, R. A., *A. E. Waite, Magician of Many Parts*, Crucible, Wellingborough, 1987. A detailed and sympathetic biography of this influential magician and mystic; explains that Waite's individual style of writing is due to his self-education, a fact that makes his scholarship and influence all the more remarkable.
6. Stewart, R. J., *Music and the Elemental Psyche*, Aquarian Press, 1987 (UK); Inner Traditions International, Vermont (USA). Gives a full system of elemental chanting as used in our ritual examples.
7. Dee, John, *Heptarchia Mystica*: a new edition with commentary and notes: Magnum Opus Sourceworks, Edinburgh (limited edition).

8. Howe, Ellic, *The Magicians of the Golden Dawn*, Aquarian Press, 1985.
9. Regardie, I, *Foundations of Practical Magic* (and other books), Aquarian Press, Wellingborough, 1979.
10. Nygren, A., *Agape and Eros* (3 vols.), SPCK, London, 1941.
11. McGregor Mathers, S. L. (trans. and adapted), *The Book of The Sacred Magic of Abramelin the Mage*, reprinted Aquarian Press, Wellingborough, 1983.
12. Quoted in (9) above for rapid reference. Otherwise developed in Jung's collected works.
13. See (3) above: also Shepard, J., *The Tarot Trumps, Cosmos in Miniature*, Aquarian Press, Wellingborough, 1985. Summarises the main theories and history of tarot, plus giving detailed references for other works.
14. Knight, G., *The Rose Cross and the Goddess*, Aquarian Press, 1985; also *The Rosicrucinan Vault* in (4) above, by Caitlin Matthews.
15. See the Trump of The Chariot in (3) above.
16. See (2,3,5) above.

FURTHER READING

AE (George William Russell), *The Candle of Vision*, the diary of a great Celtic poet and mystic. Theosophical Publishing House, Illinois, USA, 1974.

Brennan, M., *The Stars and the Stones*, Thames & Hudson, London, 1983.

Cumont, F., *Oriental Religions in Roman Paganism*, Dover, New York, 1956.

Ferrucci, P., *What We May Be* (Psychosynthesis), Turnstone Press, Wellingborough, 1982.

Knight, G., *A History of White Magic*, Mowbray, Oxford, 1978.

Luck, G., *Arcana Mundi*, Crucible, Wellingborough, 1987. Magic and occult arts in the classical world. Essential reading.

Pagels, E., *The Gnostic Gospels*.

Raine, K., *Yeats the Initiate*, George Allen & Unwin, London, 1986.

Stirling, W., *The Canon* reprinted R.I.L.K.O., 1981, distributed by Thorsons Publishing, Wellingborough. An eccentric but profound study of sacred mathematics, geometry and structures. Had considerable (often unacknowledged) influence upon a number of derivative later books.

Santillana, G. de and Von Dechend, M., *Hamlets Mill*, David R. Godine, Boston, 1977. The most exhaustive study of the relationship between consciousness and cosmology in myth and legend.

Wind, Edgar, *Pagan Mysteries in the Renaissance*, Oxford University Press, 1980.

INDEX

Printed in the United States
86612LV00002B/1-48/A